MUSEUMS OF
YUGOSLAVIA

MUSEUMS OF
YUGOSLAVIA

Newsweek/GREAT MUSEUMS OF THE WORLD

NEW YORK, N.Y.

**GREAT MUSEUMS
OF THE WORLD**

Editorial Director—Carlo Ludovico Ragghianti

MUSEUMS OF
YUGOSLAVIA

Text by:
Dr. Dragoslav Srejović

Editor:
Oto Bihalji-Merin

American Editor:
Henry A. LaFarge

Photographs:
Dragoljub Kažić

Production:
Stjepan Filek, Dragoljub Kažić

Published by
NEWSWEEK, INC.
& ARNOLDO MONDADORI EDITORE

1st Printing 1973
2nd Printing 1977
3rd Printing 1979

ISBN: Clothbound Edition 0-88225-240-2
ISBN: Deluxe Edition 0-88225-215-1

Library of Congress Catalog Card No. 76-56055

© 1973 Mladinska Knjiga of Ljubljana

First U. S. Printing 1977

INTRODUCTION

DRAGAN M. JEREMIĆ
Professor of Esthetics, Belgrade University

Yugoslavia boasts of no single museum that can compare with the great museums of the world, such as the Louvre, the British Museum, the Uffizi Gallery or the Vatican collections. In comparison with those of other, more fortunate, wealthier lands, Yugoslavia's museums were founded much later, due not only to the centuries of Turkish domination suffered by some of its states, but also to the resulting cultural lag and relative poverty after liberation, not to speak of the storms of war, which proved particularly disastrous to art treasures assembled in any one place. It has been of course difficult to make up for this delay. Nevertheless, Yugoslavia's museums contain some remarkable collections, owing to the fact that for several millennia the people who lived on her soil experienced the same urge to create as people throughout the world. Even more, geography and history have tended to transform the country into one vast museum, whose treasures— paradoxical as this may seem—remain in large part still hidden underground, undiscovered, awaiting the systematic search of expert archaeologists, or the chance discoveries of people who dig the ground to satisfy their everyday needs, thus unearthing the primeval base of their existence.

The cultural destiny of Yugoslavia has been conditioned by her geographic position on one of the main routes that have since ancient times led from East to West, from South to North and vice versa, along the Danube, Sava, Morava and Vardar river valleys, and along the Adriatic coast. This situation has made her one of the cradles of art and one of its most resistant strongholds. Here, as in all countries with a great cultural tradition, a considerable part of its artistic legacy continues to exist outside museums, even evading all attempts to be transferred there. Often far removed from the confines of walled rooms, subsisting alone under the vault of the sky, these creations compel us to leave the centers of everyday life and set out on esthetic pilgrimages. Whether they are frescoes in out-of-the-way monasteries, like those of Milesevo and Sopoćani, or tombstones in a landscape of peculiar configuration, like the "*stećaks*" of Bosnia and Herzegovina, all these masterpieces retain their magnificence only because they remain in their natural environment, illuminated by the light of the sun. They would lose a great deal if moved to the walls of a museum and merged with other unrelated works of art, in artificial lighting and congested space.

To enjoy, for instance, the beauty of "*stećaks*" to the full, one must travel to Radimlja and embrace in one single look the throng of tombstones strewn all around the fields as if they were meteorites fallen from another planet or soldiers in parade uniform, transformed by some supernatural magic into stones covered with multicolored stains and varying ornaments. Similarly, the impression gained of the Sopoćani frescoes in the very place where they were created is infinitely greater than of the same frescoes (copies, to be sure) in a museum. Therefore the deepest appreciation of these works is the reward not of those who frequent the well-arranged collections of museums, but of those who seek them out in their original locations and contemplate them in the very place where the artist imagined and created them, taking into account both the natural environment and its transformation by human hand.

In addition to the creations of certain Renaissance masters dating from the period of Italian cultural influences along our coast, the museums of Yugoslavia include, among the masters of international rank, works by Fra Angelico, Sassetta, Giovanni Bellini, Carpaccio, Altdorfer, Jacopo Bassano, Tintoretto, Veronese, Poussin, Claude Lorrain, Rembrandt, Rigaud, Piazzetta, Tiepolo, Guardi, Gros, Corot, Monet, Pissarro, Sisley, Degas, Renoir, Bonnard, Gauguin, Utrillo, Matisse, Vlaminck and Picasso; but these works are comparatively limited in scope and number. Most of the other valuable art objects exhibited, outside of smaller objects of decorative art, are creations achieved on the soil of Yugoslavia itself. But they nevertheless constitute a rich treasure, thanks to the fact that this region has been continuously inhabited from the earliest times, as witnessed by the artifacts of the diluvial "Man of Crapina", Croatia, or by similar remains found in the Karavanken range, Slovenia. Thanks to the discovery of the Starcevo and Vinca cultures, the Neolithic art of the region was already considered of exceptional richness and importance; but the recent excavations of Lepenski Vir in the Danube gorge have shown that this art was preceded by the quite outstanding creations of pre-Neolithic art. The masterpieces of the Lepenski Vir artists, who lived some seven thousand years ago, seem to anticipate many of the characteristic features of "modern" art. Their "modernity" consists, firstly, in their double levels of reference—the representational and the symbolic, simultaneously comprising figurative elements and geometric abstraction, representational image and transcendental meaning—and secondly, in their tendency to preserve not only the natural values of the medium, but even its original shape. While the four-legged images found in Kosovo and in the Morava valley can be in a certain sense considered prototypes of Hellenic centaurs, the stone sculptures from Lepenski Vir bear formal resemblances to modern, synthetic and often deliberately primitive sculpture.

Though the age of metals is, in the field of art, chiefly marked by objects of decorative art, bearing the stamp of the various tribes which in those times either temporarily or permanently settled the present Yugoslav territory, we can find among them some works of quite unusual conception that bear comparison, both by their themes and by their imaginative execution, with the showier and more famous creations of later times, e.g. the Dupljaja Chariot, also originating from the Danube Basin. Iron Age situlas from the Alpine regions are real miracles, not only of imagination and the ability to synchronize and

10

harmonize whole groups of figures into a single whole, but also of skillful technical execution, notably for example in the exceptionally well composed situlas from Vače and Magdalenska Gora. Finally, the Illyrian reliefs—from a period when Rome was beginning to exert pressures on the life of the Balkan tribes—anticipate the essential traits of the Serbian village tombs, erected many centuries later.

The southern civilization which had begun to influence the culture of the Danube basin in the Bronze Age was Mycenae, whose golden masks bear such close resemblance to the gold mask of Trebeniste, from about a millennium later. In later times, the influences of classical antiquity flooded the Balkans from all sides: from the Aegean, from the Adriatic, from the Pontic regions, and even from the Alps; but in spite of their many imitations, the Illyrian and Thracian tribes—like the Slavs in later times—in their endeavors to preserve their independence often show a tenacious resistance to the classical ideal. Though there are some statues of classical beauty from the earlier times, like the head of a goddess from Vis, the satyr figures from Stobi, or the woman's head from Solin, we can only speak of a more abiding presence of the rational, balanced realism of antiquity from the moment when some of the highest posts in the Roman Empire had become accessible to people from the Balkans; it is to the long succession of Illyrian emperors that we owe not only the palace that Emperor Diocletian erected in his native Split, but also the splendidly sculptured head of Emperor Constantine, found near his native town of Niš. Only from that time the presence of Graeco-Roman art on Yugoslav territory means not the importation of simple and often awkward provincial copies of masterpieces produced in the metropolis, but an indigenous expression of the spirit of the age. However, in one branch of figurative art the Balkan provinces can really match the art of the metropolis; namely in mosaic, either in the floor mosaics of secular buildings, like the figures of Hunters and Dionysus from Gamzigrad, and of Orpheus from Solin, or the mural decorations of churches, like the Euphrasius basilica at Porec, whose mosaics not only date from the same time as those of Ravenna, but can fully compete with them in quality.

With the Romanesque—the first style that bears a distinctive name—the age of a continuing lag behind the leading countries of the West begins; it is also the age of unabated blending of the most varied styles, often in a symbiosis unknown to any other cultural background. On the whole, on Yugoslav territory, the Romanesque period lasts from the 11th to the 14th centuries; the Gothic, from the 14th to the 16th centuries; while the Baroque only begins toward the end of the 17th or beginning of the 18th century. Thereafter the time span was gradually reduced, and today we can safely say that the disparity between the art tendencies of the leading nations and those of Yugoslavia has completely vanished. In the cultural climate prevailing, the artists have not in the least been bothered **11** by the fact that the stylistic features they accepted and developed were often simultaneously inspired by several of the religious beliefs that for centuries represented the main spiritual forces in the area and in many respects determined the basic co-ordinates of artistic creation. Moreover, even the differences between the various Yugoslav nations, especially, those of the same religion, are not as significant as they would be, had their territories not often experienced the same historical destiny and spiritual climate.

Naturally enough, in Yugoslavia, as in all countries, certain styles assumed special local traits or characteristics (the Baroque, for instance); it seems highly typical that both Gothic and Baroque art on Yugoslav territory to a large extent lost their connotations of mysticism, almost invariably present in the examples of these styles in other regions. Besides, it appears that the most remarkable fusion of various styles was achieved where the influences were the most varied: on the Adriatic coast and its immediate hinterland, as can be seen in many cases, of which we can mention for instance the Master Buvina's carved door of Split Cathedral (inspired by Byzantine iconography, yet in its wood-carving technique close to the Romanesque), or the carved pews in the same cathedral, which in addition to Romanesque and Gothic include even Islamic elements (grid-like openings and decorative animals).

Fortunately, the esthetic value of works of art is not measured by their purity of style, but by the force of the artist's creative imagination, by the beauty and vividness of his forms, and by the quality of his technique. Thus the Master Radovan, the creator of the exceptionally beautiful portal of Trogir Cathedral, is no less a great sculptor because his work quite obviously blends Lombard Romanesque with Gothic; the same may be said of Juraj Dalmatinac, the builder and decorator of Sibenik Cathedral, who combines Flamboyant Gothic architectural elements and ornamentation with certain Renaissance tendencies in sculpture, particularly in the treatment of the human figure. In the case of minor and less brilliant artists this attitude might be called eclecticism; but this term is quite unsuitable when speaking of artists like Radovan or Juraj, with whom this approach was a deliberate recognition of the limitations of the various styles, and an expression of their own creative affinities and conceptions.

The criterion of originality is certainly most difficult to defend in the case of medieval mural painting, about which so much has been written, but with highly varying opinions on the national characteristics of this fundamentally Byzantine art form. The originality of its indigenous inflection in Yugoslavia, which in certain respects both geographically and historically represents a transition from pure Byzantine painting to the pre-Renaissance and early Renaissance painting of a Cimabue or a Giotto, can be seen in several important facts. First, in these frescoes, typical local people have been depicted not only in the portraits of the founders, but also in the numerous biblical personalities and saints represented. Photographs of contemporary people compared with figures in medieval frescoes—as featured in the magazine "Yugoslavia" some twenty years ago—clearly indicate that the medieval painters must have portrayed people from the region. Secondly, at a time when the local patrons of art exerted a decisive influence on the choice of contents and themes, as well as on technical details, the frescoes not only include a great number of native saints, but also correspond to events of the day (e.g. the holy warriors in Kalenić). In this respect, one of the most influential patrons was certainly Sava Nemanjić, who inspired some of the greatest frescoes (those of Mileševo and Žicá). And thirdly, in the course of time the painters, though trained in the Greek workshops of Constantinople and Thessalonika, were increasingly recruited from the native Slav population. At first the inscriptions on the frescoes were written both in Greek and in Serbian (end of 12th century), but subsequently (13th century) they appear in Serbian only, and finally even some of the more famous masters themselves were Serbian, like those from the workshop of the Metropolitan Jovan and his brother Makarije (end of 14th century). The situation in icon painting is pretty much the same, for these were usually produced by the same painters (Michael and Eutychius in the first half of the 14th century, and some time later by the masters of Decani).

Moreover, as regards fresco painting in general, the essential question is not that of their stylistic originality, but of their inherent importance. There is no doubt that the frescoes of Serbia, Macedonia and Montenegro represent the foremost surviving examples of this style of painting known to art history—this is to some extent owing to the unfortunate fact that only very few frescoes have survived in Greece and Bulgaria. The *Procession of Angels* in St. Sophia's Church, Ochrid, the *Lamentation over the Body of Christ* in Nerezi, *The Crucifixion* in St. Mary's Church, Studenica, *The Deposition from the Cross* in Mileševo, the *Birth of the Virgin Mary* in the Patriarchal Church, Peć (St. Demetrius Church), the figures of the prophets in Resava, the *Marriage of Cana* in Kalenić, and above all, the *Assumption of the Virgin* and the *Nativity of Christ* in the church of Sopoćani, are supreme masterpieces of medieval fresco painting. The frescoes of the church of Sopoćani, which was founded by King Uroš I and mark the climax of Byzantine fresco art, and are among the highest achievements of European painting in the 13th century.

But if the importance of Yugoslav fresco painting is to a certain extent overshadowed by questions about its originality, there can be no doubt about the uniqueness of an artistic phenomenon to which no equivalent can be found in any other climate, namely the "*stećaks*", or tombstones. About 50,000 have been found (and there were twice as many in the past), all of varying sizes and sculptural techniques, with the most disparate subject matter (ranging from hunting scenes and representations of the life of medieval knights, to lunar and solar symbols, and floral and decorative motifs). Dating from the end of the 12th to the end of the 15th centuries, and spread in many regions of the Yugoslav south-west, chiefly in Bosnia and Herzegovina; they represent without question the most indigenous art form on Yugoslav soil. As far as they have been preserved by popular memory, the names of the "stonesmiths" (stone-masons) and "writers" (composers of the inscriptions), as well as those of the occupants of these sepulchral dwellings (some of which contain, in fact, simplified architectural elements), indicate that they were all local people. The attempt—now mainly abandoned—to see in these tombstones an expression of the Bogumilian heresy was motivated by the fact that the "*stećaks*" are so evidently indigenous that the only possible explanation seems to be some specific trait of Bosnian history, of which the Bogumilian heresy is certainly the most characteristic.

Since medieval times, another characteristic feature has been the emigration of artists from our territory into foreign countries inhabited by coreligionists, often linguistically related. The medieval carvers and painters frequently set out through Moldavia for distant Russia, pursuing their work there. The custom of the medieval artist not to glorify his own name in his works, prevents us from identifying these migrants. During the Renaissance, however, this habit changed radically, so that we can stress, not without a certain pride, that in addition to the artists who worked exclusively in their own country such as Nikola Božidarević and Mihoč Hamzić, a considerable number were active and became known in the outside world, facing competition much stronger than that of their fellow-countrymen: sculptors like Frano Vranjanin and Ivan Duknović, painters like Juraj Čulinović and Andrija Medulić, the miniaturist Julije Klović, and others. Vranjanin's sculptures, especially his female busts notable for their psychological penetration—soft and evanescent as if they had emerged from a dream—belong to the best achievements of the Quattrocento and can be admired in the collections of the Louvre, New York's Metropolitan Museum and Vienna's Kunsthistorisches Museum. And Medulić, by his interpretation of light, his rendering of atmosphere and his treatment of pictorial matter, was no doubt a predecessor of Tintoretto, Bassano and El Greco (whose teacher Klović, ie. Giulio Clovio, was Europe's last great miniaturist).

The Baroque, Neoclassical, Romantic and Realistic movements (and to some extent even Impressionism) in most Yugoslav regions were interpreted only by artists of historical and local importance. The Baroque style was mainly restricted to the Catholic elements of the country, while Romanticism and Realism were to a large extent inspired by the German masters of Vienna and Munich; later, the mecca of Yugoslav artists moved to Paris. For today's artists, however, the center of the world is not in any one place on the globe, but in themselves or in traditions of their own national culture. Among the artists leaning on tradition, most are trying to revive certain elements of medieval frescoes or symbols from the "*stećaks*", and at least in the opinion of foreign experts, their endeavors have not been in vain. Among those who follow their own feelings, a special place must be granted to the "naive" painters and sculptors, whose great number and high level of achievement is one of the outstanding features of contemporary Yugoslav art, which seems in this respect surpassed only by French "naïve" art. Therefore it is no wonder that Yugoslavia abounds in museums devoted exclusively to the creations of these "primitive" artists. There are several schools of this art, whose members are at the same time farmers and serious artists, and most are named after the village where they live and work (the Hlebine school, the Kovačica group, the Uzdin group of women-painters, the Oparić group, the Žiri group, etc.); probably the foremost in this art form are Ivan Generalić, among the painters, and Bogosav Živković, among the sculptors.

If we cast a final look back on the seven thousand years of artistic production on Yugoslav soil, we can find, out of the mass of individuals, schools and styles, a few artists who, pursuing some dream of their own or plunging into the realities of life, have succeeded in convincingly embodying their dream, or authentically expressing their way of life in some permanent form. From today's standpoint, more favorable to the instinctive and primitive than to the rational and academic, it appears that the greatest achievements are those of the artists from Lepenski Vir, the painters of the Ochrid icons, the masters of the frescoes of Sopoćani and Mileševo, the "stonesmiths" of the *stećaks* (Grubač, Miogost, Radić, Pribil Bjelopčelanin), the Renaissance artists Vranjanin and Medulić, the Slovenian Impressionists, and some of the naive painters of our times. Their works, in addition to Diocletian's Palace, the amphitheatre of Pula, St. Donat's Church of Zadar, and the medieval monasteries of Studenica, Dečani and Kalenić, as well as the memorial sculpture of Bogdan Bogdanović, Dušan Džamonja and Drago Tršar, represent the highest artistic attainments in Yugoslav territory. Their regional dispersions is what makes it worthwhile to visit not only Yugoslavia's museums, but the entire country. For though shaken by innumerable storms from prehistory to our own day, the whole country becomes like one great museum, still in the process of discovery and formation, continually adding to its treasures, which are too extensive to be confined within the walls of any single museum, however large.

PART I
PREHISTORY
(Tentative Image to Symbol)

PRE-NEOLITHIC ART
Sculpture No. XXXII.
Sandstone; height 17 1/4″
(The sculpture was discovered in a temple of
the pre-Neolithic fishing settlement discovered
in 1965 at Lepenski Vir in the gorge of the Danube, at the Iron Gate, on the eastern border.
Early phase of the Lepenski Vir Culture, stra-
tum Lepenski Vir II).
Belgrade, Archaeological Collection of the University

PRE-NEOLITHIC ART. *Sculpture No. XXXII.*

This large monolith from Lepenski Vir, synthesizing the form of a head with a long neck, exemplifies a prototype of monumental sculpture in Europe. It reflects the level of a highly organized prehistoric culture (the Lepenski Vir Culture) attained in the course of the 6th millennium B.C. on the banks of the Danube, in the impenetrable wilderness of the Danube Gorge.

The Lepenski Vir sculptor is obsessed by the natural shape of the round stone, seeing in it the genesis of the organic world, the first-fruit of nature born of the embrace between the large river and the stony bank—a giant egg filled with in-numerable beings striving to break out of its shell, to begin an independent ex-istence, to spring alive. The artist arrives at the image desired by the simplest means: he merely breaks the surface of the stone in a few places, and without any serious intrusions into its depth liberates an impressive figure from its core. The basic conception of this sculpture is distinctly relief-like, and the technique used is reminiscent of wood-carving—a method rediscovered in our time by Brancusi, who applied it to stone-carving in the belief that it was the best way of animating crude matter. A form created on this principle is endowed with an intense vital force, for the tensions of inner energies are not equally transposed on the outer surfaces: they are concentrated only in a few outstanding points. The artist seems to be aware that sensual perception cannot discover the es-sence of things, and that only beneath the visible surfaces, somewhere deep in-side the stone, can be guessed the veins and arteries along which the living sub-stance of the form flows and pulsates.

PRE-NEOLITHIC ART. *Deer in a Forest.* p. 20

This *Deer in a Forest* is one of the later creations of the Lepenski Vir Culture. On a large round stone the artist carved a maze of deep incisions, capturing some meaning of the real world essential to him. But what is the meaning?

The curving furrows, some long, others short, run along the surface of the stone, converging, breaking off, suddenly reappearing, but in spite of their live-ly motion never composing a definite image. The main theme remains carefully hidden in the labyrinth of entangled pathways that do not lead to any deter-mined goal. The image does not seem transposed on the surfaces according to any predetermined concept, yet apparently grows in the actual process of sculpturing: the furrows follow the outlines of the monolith, by-pass its pro-truding spots, descend into its concavities, and follow the natural veins of the stone. As a final result, an abstract form is achieved that possesses a miracu-lous power of transformation.

This sculpture unquestionably purports to represent a determined subject bor-rowed from nature, and it is only because of its intricacy that this subject, in the course of its figurative concretization, has been utterly rationalized, sche-matized and transformed into abstract form. Did the artist actually seek to de-pict a deer in a forest? This is probably only a deceptive impression, for every repeated encounter with this form reveals that any previous impression about it was wrong. It is certain, however, that the complete negation of objective figu-ration proves neither simplicity of subject matter, nor primitiveness of execu-tion, but on the contrary, the extreme intricacy and subtlety of the theme con-ceived.

PRE-NEOLITHIC ART
Deer in a Forest
6th millennium B.C.
Sandstone; height 23 5/8″
(The large monolith, covered by arabesques possibly conveying the figure of a deer, comes from a structure in the pre-Neolithic settlement of Lepenski Vir II. Early phase of the Lepenski Vir Culture).
Belgrade, Archaeological Collection of the University

PRE-NEOLITHIC ART
Man with Plaited Hair
6th millennium B.C.
Sandstone; height 14 1/8″
(Human face with fish-like traits, framed by ornaments recalling long plaits or possibly the scales of a fish. This sculpture was found in the pre-Neolithic settlement of Lepenski Vir II. Early phase of the Lepenski Vir Culture).
Belgrade, Archaeological Collection of the University

PRE-NEOLITHIC ART.   *Man with Plaited Hair.*
The sculpture entitled *Man with Plaited Hair* dates from near the end of the 6th millennium B.C., at a time when the Lepenski Vir Culture was dying out. It represents a human figure enclosed within the frame of the immutable stone block, without any organic breaks and without any single free, asymmetrically placed detail. Because of this insistence on symmetry, the image as a whole is in a certain sense dematerialized.

The body of the figure is hidden behind a crudely modelled cloak. Two distinctly symmetrical ornamental motifs—the interlace and the chevron—cover the figure in uninterrupted parallel strings, delimit the face, disguise the borderlines between the covered and the nude surfaces of the body, link the unorganic with the organic, and level what is felt as motionless and permanent with what is alive and transitory. The eyes, the nose, the mouth and the triangular contour of the chin are not contrasted with this geometrical scheme, but included in it, placed along the paths of the ornamental motifs and stylized according to their forms: the round eyes are only enlarged loops of the interlace, while the sharp outlines of the chin and the drooping mouth simply imitate the angular incisions that form the chevrons. The figure seems to be, just like the ornament, incorporeal, deprived of any organic life or free movement; but just like the chevrons and the interlace, it is distinguished by its perfect determinateness.

ART OF THE LOWER NEOLITHIC. *Beaker with Necklace.*

This vessel, containing a valuable necklace of spondyl and buccinum shells, bone and paligorskite, was unearthed in the settlement of Lepenski Vir III b, erected towards the first half of the 5th millennium B.C., at a time of stabilized lower Neolithic culture (later phase of the Starčevo Culture).

The precious materials used in the beads of the necklace (the Mediterranean shell called spondylus, and the exceptionally rare mineral named paligorskite, whose only known sites are in the Urals and in Anatolia) prove that the inhabitants of the central Danube basin had at that time already established contacts with the distant regions of the Mediterranean and the Middle East. These new routes of travel and the exchanges of goods along them must have evoked images of distant lands and new worlds with strange landscapes and beings. That they excited the mind of primitive man and gave flight to his fancy is shown by the zoömorphous pendant that crowns the necklace and represents an imaginary, fantastic animal with an elongated, winding neck, a protruding muzzle and strange horn-like excrescences on its head.

The same purpose seems to have dictated the incisions on the vase in which the necklace was found. It is characteristic that these do not form a static ornamental current nor any definite motif, but interweave, chase one another, spread out and cover the whole surface restlessly.

ART OF THE LOWER NEOLITHIC
Beaker with Necklace
Middle of 5th millennium B.C.
Height of beaker 4 3/4"; length of necklace 29 1/2"
(The inhabitants of the Neolithic settlement Lepenski Vir 111b—early phase of the Starčevo Culture—used this beaker of brown-baked clay to keep the precious necklace probably imported from the Mediterranean).
Belgrade, Archaeological Collection of the University

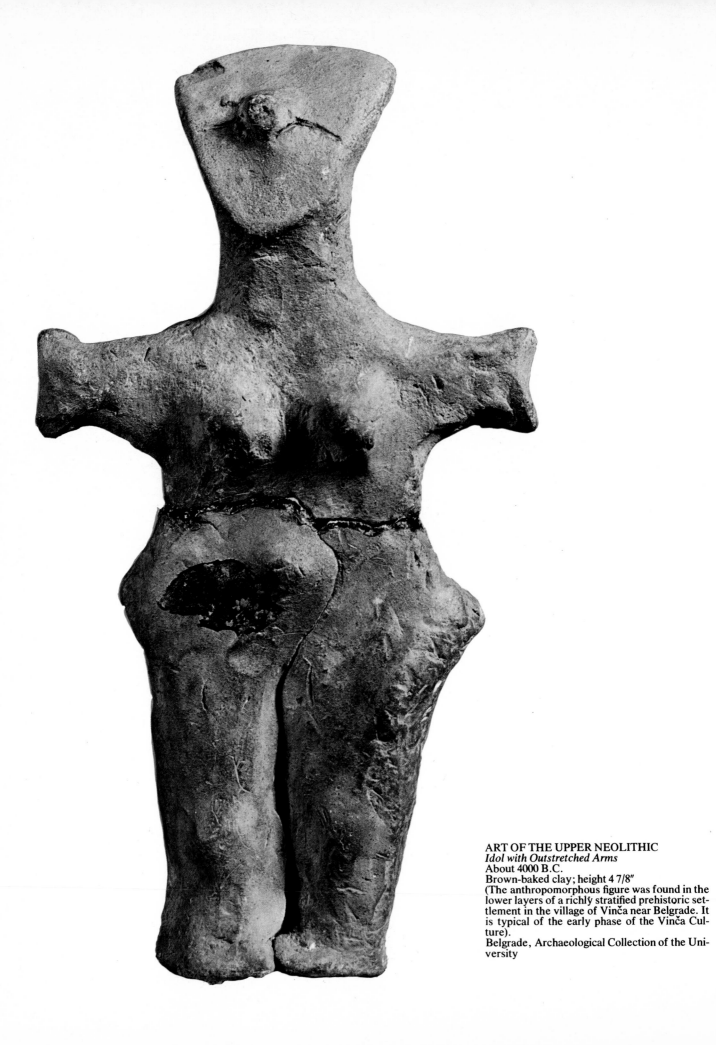

ART OF THE UPPER NEOLITHIC
Idol with Outstretched Arms
About 4000 B.C.
Brown-baked clay; height 4 7/8"
(The anthropomorphous figure was found in the
lower layers of a richly stratified prehistoric settlement in the village of Vinča near Belgrade. It
is typical of the early phase of the Vinča Culture).
Belgrade, Archaeological Collection of the University

ART OF THE EARLY MESOLITHIC
Group of Anthropomorphous Figurines
Second half of the 4th millennium B.C.
Red-baked clay; height of the figurines 7 3/8"–6"
(Group of six anthropomorphous statuettes
modelled in the linear abstract style, found in a
house of a vast prehistoric settlement discov-
ered in 1956 at Divostin near Kragujevac).
Kragujevac, National Museum

ART OF THE UPPER NEOLITHIC. *Idol with Outstretched Arms.*   p. 22

In the large, multistratal prehistoric settlement of Vinča near Belgrade—which
is one of the primary centres of upper Neolithic culture in the Danube basin
(the so-called Vinča Culture)—thousands of anthropomorphous statuettes have
been unearthed, among them this idol that clearly reflects the interests and
moods of the inhabitants of the central Danube regions at the beginning of a
new and long-lasting stage of prehistory.

The nude human figure with its extended arms, proudly uplifted head and realistically modelled body conveys the almost childish joy of the artist, who succeeded in creating a dynamic form out of the soft clay. For this artist, the body
hides no secrets: the arms stand out from the main mass, the long, elegant neck
is drawn out, the breasts, thighs and buttocks are well modelled, and the legs
with the knees and feet firmly indicated seem ready to step forward. The outlines are harsh and the anatomic structure of the figure is crude, but the human
figure as a whole is given natural proportions.

The contrast between the realistically modelled body and the schematized head
is a new element combining the traditional abstraction of form with a new stylistic conception, which towards the end of the 5th millennium B.C. had arrived
from Anatolia to the continental regions of the Balkans. It is, however, certain
that this tendency towards realism was not entirely inspired by foreign influences. The artist himself must have had plenty of reasons to approach life with
confidence, to endeavor to reproduce the forms found in nature faithfully.

ART OF THE EARLY MESOLITHIC. *Group of Anthropomorphous Figurines* *p. 23*

ART OF THE UPPER NEOLITHIC
Dish with Spirals in Relief
First half of the 4th millennium B.C.
Red-baked clay; height 5 3/4"
(The dish comes from the Neolithic settlement
of Nebo in the Bila Valley, Bosnia. It is typical
of the Butimir Culture of the upper Neolithic).
Sarajevo, Regional Museum

In the large prehistoric settlements of Divostin, six anthropomorphous figurines of unequal sizes, but almost identical in form come from the ruins of a hut.

All the figurines are characterized by a peculiar type of head, bird-like in appearance, and a linearly schematized body. This form seems to have resulted from a systematic reduction of older, more realistically modelled forms. On these bird-faces the cheekbones are connected with the chin, long nose and oblique eyes into a single mass, standing out from the level of forehead and neck. The body is modelled in a similar way: the abdominal section, from navel to hips, is set at an oblique angle to the conjoined legs, which are fused together and relegated to a separate mass. By arranging the masses into various planes, the impression of special modelling is achieved. Seen as a whole, the figurines are very bird-like; but this is an image frequent in prehistoric art, and implies simultaneously the forces of life and death.

The figurines from Divostin were created by a generation that marked the close of the Vinča Culture. This generation lived without any contacts with the outside world, for it was encircled by encroaching cultures of the late Mesolithic and the early Bronze Age. As its members lost faith in their own forces, they relied increasingly on assistance from supernatural powers. This assistance, however, was as impersonal and abstract as the figures of their idols.

ART OF THE UPPER NEOLITHIC. *Dish with Spirals in Relief.*   *p. 24*
This large dish from Nebo, profusely decorated with spirals in relief, dates from the middle of the 4th millennium B.C., a time when the Neolithic culture of the Balkans reached its zenith. It was a period of effervescent life, when peace was established throughout Europe.

The Nebo potter contrasts the inarticulate form of the vessel with the complicated relief ornament of interconnected S-formed spirals. The morphology of this curvilinear ornament is rational and clear; but with no point of departure or arrival, it seems endowed, like life itself, with the power of continual regeneration. The ground remains clearly perceptible, but is flat and inert, offering no resistance to the will of the ornamental stream, and only serving to accentuate the dynamic rhythm of the plastic decoration in its striving for the conquest of all the space available. By setting the agitated meander against the calm and monotonous surface, the contrast between living and dead matter stands out in full relief, and the endless repetition of the basic motif seems to intimate the infinity of time and space. With emphasis laid on the plastic spiral, the form expresses hopeful vitality, a symbol of life vigorously divorced from its base, and triumphant over dead matter.

ART OF THE UPPER NEOLITHIC. *Woman with a Dish.*
In contrast to the anthropomorphous figurines of the lower Neolithic, always impersonal, nude, without sexual signs or attributes, the *Woman with a Dish* is iconographically clearly defined; it proves that by the first half of the 4th millennium B.C. the archetypal image of the Great Mother had already been for-

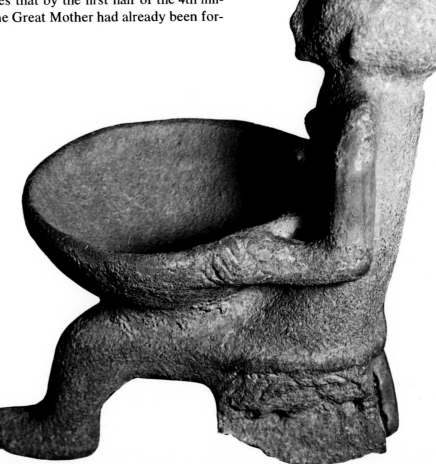

ART OF THE UPPER NEOLITHIC
Woman with a Dish
First half of the 4th millennium B.C.
Red-baked clay with white coating; height 7 5/8″
(The figurine was accidentally found near Becej, Banat, in a place where potsherds of the Tisza Culture have been excavated since).

ART OF THE EARLY MESOLITHIC
Human Head
Second half of the 4th millennium B.C.
Brown-baked clay; height 6 7/8″
(This stylized human head from Predionica is a
masterpiece of European art of the early Meso-
lithic).
Prishtina, Museum of Kosovo and Metohija

ART OF THE EARLY MESOLITHIC
Seated Anthropomorphous Figurine
Second half of the 4th millennium B.C.
Red-baked clay; height of the figurine 7 1/4″
(This human figure seated on a throne, mod-
elled in the ornamental style, was discovered at
Predionica near Prishtina, together with materi-
als characteristic of the early phase of the Vin-
ca Culture).
26   Prishtina, Museum of Kosovo and Metohija

mulated, and that man had arrived at the stage of significant symbols and as-
sociated thoughts.

This figurine from Bordjoš combines three distinct elements into a single
whole: the naked female body, the dish and the throne. By the realistic modelling of the head and the emphasis on the breasts, the image of the Great Mother
attains definite attributes: the breasts emphasize her role as universal nourish-
er, while the head with the deeply set eyes and large mouth points toward her
demonic, negative powers and her connection with the darkness of the underground world. The large dish is a symbol with clearly established meanings:
closely connected with the woman's body and laid in her lap, it quite evidently
signifies the womb, this inexhaustible source of life.

The nude female figure, the dish and the throne are complementary symbols,
by which the Neolithic artist defines the image of the "eternal woman."

EARLY MESOLITHIC ART.   *Seated Anthropomorphous Figurine.*   p. 27
This figurine from Predionica is modelled in the Ornamental Style. The free-
standing figure is unnaturally flattened, with little or no attention given to profile. By this procedure, the frontal view of the figure is emphasized, and large
flat surfaces have been obtained that can accept an incised design. The incisions do not represent any determined details, but merely enliven the surfaces
and serve to intimate forms that cannot be exactly represented in a two-dimensionally conceived figure.

The majestic pose, the symmetry and the pronounced frontality give this figurine an impressive appearance. The basic accent is not set on sensual perception, but on a subjective idea of the object represented; the observer's eyes
only fleetingly dwell on the human figure, and are then immediately led to a series of associations linked with it, which elevate the contemplated form to the
level of a general idea and unalterable symbol. This concept of form, introvert-
ed and practically transcendental, could only have arisen out of a mood of extreme restlessness and fears about events in the outside world.

EARLY MESOLITHIC ART.   *Human Head.*
The basic principles of the Ornamental Style, born out of the concept of the
world peculiar to the last generations of peaceful farmers and cattle-breeders in
the continental regions of the Balkans, achieve their most perfect expression in
this monumental head from Predionica.

The human head is two-dimensionally conceived and modelled like a relief image. The large, empty eyes, diagonally placed, and the pronounced plane of the
forehead which extends down into nose and chin in a vertical line, are underlined by incisions forming the scheme of a quadri-segmented cross in the triangular face. The head as a whole gives the effect of a terrifying, immobile mask,
as if to disguise the real identity of the person represented. This "masquerade"
is not connected with any ritual play, neither does it represent tattooing or a
means by which primitive man tries to impress his enemies; it is simply a faithful rendering of the psychology of an anxious generation, unprepared to accept
the more highly developed economic and social structure and the new gods already reigning in the culture of the neighboring regions.

ART OF THE LATE MESOLITHIC. *Dove.*

This bird-form vase, with the sign of the double ax incised three times on its neck, was unearthed in the prehistoric settlement of Vučedol, in the niche of a small underground chapel, in the immediate vicinity of votive horns. Birds, the double-axe and the votive horns—these are the three most important religious symbols of the Aegean culture of the Bronze Age. They show that the Vučedol Culture came from the same roots as the Cycladic, Minoan and Helladic cultures and that its point of departure can be traced back to the late Chalcolithic culture of Anatolia (Beyce-Sultan).

The potter of Vučedol is apparently uninterested in the actual appearance of the bird; he sets his "dove" on three feet, gives her unnatural proportions, covers her body with geometrical motifs, and gives her four eyes. But this is only a setting for the sign of the double-axe incised in her neck, and it is this mysterious symbol which gives a sense to the entire image. The double-axe consists of two triangles closely interlinked at their peaks—the male and female principles combined into one active whole, the sign of lightning connecting heaven and earth, or some other secret, untranslatable message.

ART OF THE LATE MESOLITHIC
Dove
First half of the 3rd millennium B.C.
Gray-baked clay; height 7 5/8"
(The sculptural bird-form vase, embellished with incised ornament with white incrustation, was found in Vučedol, Slavonia, in the niche of an underground temple).
Zagreb, Archaeological Museum

ART OF THE BRONZE AGE
Idol with Bell-Skirt
Second half of the 2nd millennium B.C.
Brown-baked clay; height 5 3/8"
(The stylized anthropomorphous figurine was found in a tomb of the huge incineration necropolis at Korbovo, Eastern Serbia. The incised ornament is incrusted with white paint).
Belgrade, National Museum

ART OF THE BRONZE AGE.   *Idol with Bell-Skirt.*

This idol with a bell-shaped skirt, on which only the picturesque details of dress are emphasized while the human figure itself is deprived of all anatomic details and reduced to a symbolic formula, was found in the Danube basin, near the village of Korbovo.

In contrast to the "baroque" modelling of form in the earlier phases of the Bronze Age, the *Idol from Korbovo* marks a new, "rococo" phase in the stylistic development of prehistoric art in the Danube basin. The artist is only interested in the rich ornamentation representing embroidery on the dress and the glitter of the jewellery on the torso. He submits to all that is sensuous and beautiful, he is charmed by the subtle interlacing of trellis-like curves on the large surfaces, and has thus become a virtuoso decorator, somewhat superficial, but with a highly refined taste. In contemplating this figurine, we are left with the impression that the bearers of late Bronze Age culture in the central Danube even in actual life preferred idleness, precious jewellery and lavishly embroidered textiles to devoted labor, discipline and success in battle. The *Idol from Korbovo* indicates a primitive exaltation of everything sumptuous and pretty.   **29**

ART OF THE BRONZE AGE. *Ritual Carriage.*

The discovery of bronze caused not only an economic, but also a great spiritual upheaval throughout the regions of Central and South-East Europe in the first centuries of the 3rd millennium B.C. With the gradual development of metallurgy, the people of Europe soon found themselves freed from absolute attachment to the soil and dependency on narrow tribal communities. The search for sources of the metal, its processing, transportation and possession gave those involved a special prominence within the social structure of the Bronze Age— the discoverers, craftsmen, merchants and warriors, people of daring and imagination, rich in experience and always ready for action. The world became a large and dynamic place, attractive, but at the same time terrifying, full of enigmas which the human mind, despite all the dangers involved, tried to work out.

The *Ritual Carriage,* created in the 2nd millennium B.C., gives a faithful picture of this new world of bronze. A basket-shaped wagon, with three large wheels and a pair of shafts whose ends are transformed into birds, is driven by an anthropomorphic figure dressed in a long robe. The bird-like head of the figurine is summarily modelled, but the details of the costume are carefully elaborated. Outward signs of sex are omitted, but beneath the hollow bell-shaped skirt a man's genitals are indicated. The artist from Dupljaja evidently intended to represent the long-robed man in a dominating pose, majestically travelling through the wide world, in a wagon drawn by a team of marsh birds. This is not a tranquil scene of departure for a long voyage, but the fixation of a moment of action. The dynamism of the composition is stressed by giving the whole group the basic form of an elongated triangle, at whose narrowed peak, in the foreground, an unnaturally large movable wheel strikes the observer's eyes. This light apex seems to break through the frame of space and to direct the much heavier masses of the background toward some distant goal. By this interplay of energies between the first and the second plane, the otherwise heterogeneous elements of the group merge firmly into a single whole, and spatial depth is specially underlined.

The artist of Dupljaja senses his masses more like a painter than as a sculptor. He is eccentric and undisciplined, too sensitive to set his figurative group decisively in space, to give it firm contours, to avoid illusionistic deformation of volumes, to neglect the contrasts of light and dark along the agitated surfaces. The figurine on the wagon therefore seems to hover in space, somewhere on the border between reality and irreality. The scene is not quite clear either in its details or as a whole, but it is precisely this complexity which provokes our curiosity. All the forms of the group appear ambiguous.

ART OF THE BRONZE AGE
Ritual Carriage
Middle of 2nd millennium B.C.
Brown-baked clay
Carriage 25.6 x 6 1/4"; anthropomorphous figurine 5 1/4"
(Anthropomorphous figurine on a carriage drawn by marsh birds. This sculptural group was accidentally found in the village of Dupljaja, near Vršac).
Belgrade, National Museum

ART OF THE BRONZE AGE
Votive Ring
End of 2nd millennium B.C.
Bronze inlaid with gold, dimensions 3 3/4″ x 4″
(Open ring, decorated with incised geometrical ornament at the widened ends, and with gold circles along its circumference, accidentally found in Drmno near the Rukomija Monastery, Eastern Serbia).
Belgrade, National Museum

ART OF THE BRONZE AGE.   *Votive Ring.*

Between 1200 and 800 B.C., incessant migrational movements, created great restlessness throughout Europe. The quiet life of the old settlements was interrupted, conflicts spread everywhere, and the laws of war and death reigned unopposed. Because of the general uncertainty, valuable objects were hidden in specified deposits or interred with the ashes of the incinerated dead. It is from one of these caches or tombs that this large bronze ring, accidentally found in Drman, Eastern Serbia, is believed to have originated.

The dimensions of the ring indicate that it could not have been used in everyday life. Its geometric decoration is directly related to the decorative styles of the sub-Mycenaean and proto-geometrical cultures of Greece. There is something frightening in the very form of this ring: it recalls a strong iron collar like a shackle, or a pair of hands with strong fists, prepared to choke and strangle. The decoration, concentrated on the flat surfaces at the two ends of the ring, is cold and geometrically rigid. The hatches that formulate triangles, parallel lines, zig-zag patterns, concentric circles and garlands, are strictly organized into friezes and metopes, while the monotony of the rounded surfaces is broken only by four circular sockets inlaid with gold. This geometric style of the Northern Balkans, like the new custom of incinerating the dead, renounces all that is organic and changeable, and faithfully reflects the prevailing atmosphere of hopelessness and fear.

ART OF THE LOWER IRON AGE
Ascus Jars, with Cups
First half of 1st millennium B.C.
Red-baked clay
Height of jars 6 5/8″ and 6 1/8″; height of cups
2 3/4″ and 2 5/8″
(These ascus jars with cups were found in the
large incineration necropolis of Dalj, Baranja.
On their glossy red surface are faintly visible
ornaments—possibly meanders—painted red).
Zagreb, Archaeological Museum

ART OF THE LOWER IRON AGE. *Ascus Jars, with Cups.*

After the centuries of migrational waves, spreading by a kind of chain reaction
from the Danube basin to Greece, Asia Minor and Egypt, a truce was at last established about 800 B.C. in the continental regions of Europe; it was during this
lull that the Scythian, Thracian, Illyrian and Celtic ethnic groups were definite-
ly formed and the last great styles of prehistoric art born. These ascus-formed
jars and cups from Dalj indicate that the new Lower Iron Age style in the Danube basin sprang out of a combination of traditional forms with elements imported from Thraco-Cimmerian, Scythian, Italic and Greek cultures.

The forms of the Dalj vases imitate the precious, sumptuously decorated vessels of silver and gold produced between the 9th and 6th centuries B.C. in Iran.
These vessels were copied by both Scyths, Cimmerians and Greeks, and often
reproduced in clay. On their long voyage from Luristan to the central Danube
the basic patterns underwent considerable modifications, and instead of the
original complex scenes with fantastic beings the jars and cups from Dalj only
represent the stylized heads of Danubian birds and the figures of animals from
the Pannonian grazing grounds. The local master filled the surfaces of the vases
with meanders, and thus linked the traditional geometric style of the Balkans
with Eastern Mediterranean figuration.

ART OF THE LOWER IRON AGE.   *Situla from Vače.*

By the fusion of three components—Oriental, Graeco-Italic and Central European—one of the great masterpieces of prehistoric art was created about 500 B.C.: the *Vače Situla.* This bronze vessel with its luxurious figurative decoration was found by a farmer in 1883, in a place where an Iron Age settlement with an extensive necropolis was subsequently excavated.

The outward form of the situla is simple. It is a conic pail with sharply profiled shoulder, short neck and round rim. The lively relief decoration, achieved by the technique of hammering, is arranged in three friezes on this calm, clearly articulated form. The upper frieze represents on one side of the situla a solemn procession of horsemen, and on the opposite side a race of war chariots. In the central frieze, beneath the parade of horsemen, four scenes of sacrifice are pictured, with men presenting incense, food and drink to their throning ancestors, while the opposite side features four observers witnessing a combat between two naked wrestlers. The third, lowest frieze shows a peaceful sequence of wild goats and deer.

In spite of the clear dividing lines, both along the horizontal (ribs in relief) and along the vertical planes (rivets connecting the sections of metallic plate), all the scenes are conceptually and figuratively related. While the figures of the upper frieze move from right to left, and those of the lower frieze from left to right, the central frieze is arranged in symmetrical groups, which harmonize the two opposing rhythms and equilibrate the entire composition. The scenes represented in the upper and central friezes on each side of the situla are iconographically connected: the festive procession of horsemen with the scene of sacrifice, and the chariot race with the scene of wrestling for a shield. The lower frieze seems independent and continuous, but it is apparently not of a purely decorative character, for on the same side where the deceased ancestors are represented, a lion is shown devouring another animal, while beneath the race and the wrestling match only a quiet procession of wild goats and deer is seen. Evidently, the side of the situla representing the competitors stands for light, life and its joys, while the opposite side, with its solemn rites, including the central scene of sacrifice, belongs to death. There are no sharp borderlines between these two worlds, for all the actions represented refer to the glorification of ancestors, who are pictured in what is certainly the main scene of the situla, calmly sitting on their thrones in eternal bliss.

This narrative and figurative idiom belongs to the Eastern Mediterranean. But everything else—the form of the vessel, the technique of hammered bronze plate, the rhythm and structure of the composition—is linked to the traditions of Central European art. The realistic forms of the Eastern Mediterranean, transferred through the mediation of Greeks and Etrurians to Northern Italy as early as the beginning of the 6th century B.C. (the Benvenuti Situla), were blended in the Veneto-Alpine region with the local geometric style. In this new figurative synthesis the solidity of the figures is only superficially retained as a primary value. Certain organic forms are overemphasized, all attention is concentrated on the details, and only one important feature of every single figure or situation is underlined. This digression from reality is even more emphasized by the continuing presence of the traditional geometrical scheme, clearly felt both in the rigid limitation of space and in the structure of the composition. By this fusion of Mediterranean realism and the traditional abstraction of Central Europe, a highly original figurative synthesis has been achieved.

ART OF THE LOWER IRON AGE
Situla from Vače
About 500 B.C.
Bronze plate joined by rivets, height 9 3/8" without handle
(The situla was accidentally found in 1883 in the mountain village of Vače near Litija, Slovenia. The upper and central friezes show various scenes with human and animal figures, rendered by the technique of hammering; the lower frieze represents a procession of animals).
Ljubljana, National Museum

34

ART OF THE LOWER IRON AGE
Situla from Vače
Detail of the central frieze.

ART OF THE LOWER IRON AGE. *Gold Mask.* *p. 38*

This mask of hammered gold plate, found in 1930 in tomb No. 8 of the necropolis excavated near Trebenište, was produced in the last decades of the 6th century B.C., to immortalize the features of a deceased Illyrian chieftain.

The man's face, with its long, prominent nose, thick eyebrows, closed eyes, protruding cheekbones and thin, compressed lips, seems almost to have been cast directly from the dead body. Not even death was able to efface his virility, decision and courage. Such individualized figuration, modelled like a portrait, is otherwise unknown in European art of the 6th century; but it is well known from the gold masks of Mycenae of about a thousand years earlier. This seems to imply that the Trebenište mask is the work of a local artist, and that it originated in an Illyrian environment, which with its fortified settlements, its rich royal tombs and its social structure based on military autocracy closely resembled the heroic world of Homer's epics. Only by this similarity of social and economic conditions the remarkable revival of Mycenaean culture at the end of the 6th century in the guise of a distinct Illyrian artistic style can be satisfactorily explained. This vigorous and exalted mode became a permanent spiritual possession of the inhabitants of the Balkans, and throughout their later history continued to reappear whenever their national traditions, rights and dignity were at stake. So the face of the chieftain on the golden mask of Trebenište can be met again in Roman times, on native tombstones, then on the medieval "stećaks" of the 13th–16th centuries, and finally in our own day, on the memorial stones spread along the village lanes.

ART OF THE LOWER IRON AGE
Gold Mask
About 520 B.C.
Hammered gold plate, dimensions 6 7/8″ x 7 1/4″
(This gold mask of the face of a dead man is naturalistically modelled, but framed with an abstract network. It was found in the Illyrian necropolis near Trebeniste, Macedonia, among other precious objects).
Belgrade, National Museum

PART II
ANTIQUITY
(Real to Transcendental Forms)

GREEK ARCHAIC ART
Bronze Crater
Detail of frieze with horsemen.

GREEK ARCHAIC ART
Bronze Crater
Circa 520 B.C.
Bronze plate; height 28 3/8"
(This crater with volute-shaped handles, found in 1930 near Trebeniŝte, in the chieftain's tomb No. VIII, is decorated with four horsemen and two Medusas, while its tripod shows three Medusas, three dogs and three foxes).
Belgrade, National Museum

GREEK ARCHAIC ART. *Bronze Crater.*

This bronze crater with volute-shaped handles and tripod, discovered in 1930 in the Illyrian necropolis near Trebeniŝte, is unquestionably—along with the famous crater from Vix—the most perfect example of archaic Greek metalwork.

The *Crater from Trebeniŝte* combines, on a reduced scale, everything that Greek monumental art had achieved up to the last decades of the 6th century B.C. By its balanced structure, its harmonious proportions of masses, its frieze and its sumptuous decoration, the *Crater* is related to the Attic-Ionian architecture of the second half of the 6th century B.C., while its figurative decoration, which blends in an ideal way elements of the Doric and Ionic styles, is related to the contemporary painting and sculpture of Athens, Argos and Euboea.

The figurative decoration is restricted to the neck of the crater (four horsemen, two Medusas) and the tripod support (three Medusas flanked by a dog and a fox), while the ornamentation (palmettes, volutes, astragals, cymas) is limited to the rim and foot of the vessel. The largest, central surface of the crater is left unadorned, emphasizing the overall shape of the vase. The frontally represented, static and terror-producing Medusa figures contrasted with the galloping horsemen, who are shown boldly turning with smiling faces towards the observer. This contrast instills the scene on the frieze with so much life that at first sight the harshly modelled details are overlooked: the geometrical incisions in the horsemen's hair, the crudely indicated muscles of their bodies, and the unnatural pose of their heads. But these limitations are abundantly compensated by the remarkable foreshortenings and indications of depth, which endow the figures with volume, while the very air around seems to envelope them. The workshop in which the *Crater from Trebeniŝte* was produced has not yet been established. Earlier suppositions that this bronze vessel originates

from Corinthian, Argive or Lacedaemonian workshops lack probability. The artistic production of Corinth and other Dorian towns had died out about the middle of the 6th century B.C., and from then on Chalcis and Eritraea had taken the lead, happily connecting in their workshops the best features of thé Ionic and Doric styles.

GREEK VASE PAINTING. *Hydria in the Red-Figure Style.*

At a time when the best forces of Greece were being wasted in the Pelopennesian wars, while in the streets of Athens the Sophists were calling in doubt the significance of ancient religion, and in the theatres the public was guffawing at the exaggerations of Aristophanes and shedding tears at the tragedies of Euripides, a certain Meidias, or one of his closest collaborators, painted this hydria found in a tomb near Demir-Kapija.

Neither the echoes of the precarious economic situation, nor the repeated defeats of Athens, nor the general psychological tension of the last decades of the 5th century B.C. are reflected in the decoration of this vase. The painter has represented Dionysus, god of mirth and fertility, surrounded by a merry procession of Meanads and Erotes offering the voluptuous joys of life.

On this vase style reigns supreme. Tradition and artistic routine allow the painter to retain his balance of composition, avoiding any nervous rhythms and apparently regaining the classic serenity of a Phidias. Dionysus and a Maenad are represented sitting calmly in the centre, while the figures surrounding them are shown in lively motion: on one side two Maenads, on the other side Eros and a Maenad with a deer. Beneath the main scene, but not on the same axis, a similar symmetrical group appears, consisting of two seated Maenads flanked by Eros and a Maenad in motion. These two parallel currents, though rhythmically interrupted, repeat the same regularity and pronounced symmetry. Monotony is also evaded along the vertical line. The figures are set in a step-like arrangement, on various levels, as if the scene were happening on sloping ground. This method of indicating perspective is a feature of the much earlier paintings of Polygnotus. Apparently Meidias had no occasion to copy the works of his contemporaries Apollodorus and Agatharchus, who introduced shadows and genuine perspective in painting; he still draws on tradition, and most successfully imitates the works of monumental sculpture.

The vase painting of the last decade of the 5th century is quite as decorative and elegant as the architecture of the Erechtheum or the temple of Nike Apteros, and the sculpture of Kallimachus. Far removed from painful and ugly reality, this is a world of daydreams in careless idleness, of ostentatious display of wealth, of brilliant external effects.

GREEK VASE PAINTING OF
THE FIFTH CENTURY
Maenad
Detail from the hydria in the red-figure style.

43

HELLENISTIC ART
Piping Satyr
1st century B.C.
Hollow cast bronze; height 3'8"
(This Satyr comes from Stobi, Macedonia).
Belgrade, National Museum

GREEK ARCHAIC ART
Maenad
Circa 500 B.C.
Massive cast bronze; height 3 3/4"
(This Maenad was found in a large rectangular
walled tomb. It was probably intended to deco-
rate the rim of a bronze dish).
Skopje, Archaeological Museum

GREEK ARCHAIC ART. *Maenad.*

This *Maenad* from Tetovo was undoubtedly part of a figurative group decorating the rim of a large bronze wine vessel. She is represented in flight, with raised hands, looking back, probably towards her pursuer, Silenus. The joyful expression of her face and coquettish gestures clearly indicate that it is all a game. The figure is perfectly suited to a wine vessel and to the mood of the participants in a feast.

The love of picturesque detail, the explicit story-telling pose and the sudden motion are characteristic of the Ionian-Attic art of the middle of the 6th century B.C., but the proportions of the Maenad's body, her oversize head with stylized hair and her frontally positioned torso and the feet set in profile are reminiscent of the much earlier works of the Archaic period. These contrasts are also apparent in the drapery: the folds of the upper part of the chiton are indicated by parallel wave-like incisions, as on the vases of the painter Amasis, while those of the lower part, beneath the harshly modelled nebris, are quite linear and lifeless. By this conscious archaicism, Greek art of the late 6th century marks a return to firmer modelling, fuller forms, greater clarity and symmetry.

HELLENISTIC ART. *Piping Satyr.* *p. 45*

About the time Socrates convinced the painter Parasius that any mood could be expressed on the faces and in the poses of figures, from deepest pain to elated mirth, Greek art began to experience a sharp turn towards the cultivation of sentiment and emphasis on purely sensual perception. While the sculptors of the 4th century B.C. (Praxiteles, Lysippus, Apelles) still succeeded in representing emotional content with restraint, in the later Hellenistic period excessive interest in all that is sensual and effective led to the creation of genre scenes, figuratively interesting, but empty behind their lively forms.

Thematically this bronze *Satyr* from Stobi is linked to the Hellenistic art cultivated in Alexandria. But formally, by its proportions, restrained motion, nobly rendered muscles and theatrically uplifted head, the figure is still close to sculpture of the 4th century. The mass of the body is retained as the highest value; all attention is focused on the hands, in the long, playing fingers that extract an exciting melody from the pipe. The sounds dim the Satyr's eyes, stream through his body, and prepare it for the ecstasy of dance. The legend about the gay, dissolute follower of the god Dionysus is soon forgotten; the diminutive tail on his back, the stumpy nose and the curly hair are hardly noticed, and only the impression of inspired piping remains, its rhythm cast in bronze.

ROMAN ART. *Head of a Young Woman.*

The *Head of a Young Woman* from Salona (Solin), with its complicated, but dignified hairdress, softly modelled face and large eyes, contrasted with the small mouth and the shortened, receding chin, express mildness and resigned sadness. The tense surfaces of the cheeks and forehead are contrasted with the shadowed mass of the hair, stressing the almost painful paleness of the face. Without display, without emphasizing her charms, the young woman seems to be contemplating life in a mood of resignation. The modelling is restrained, the attention is concentrated on the deeper planes of the form, and the only power this face appears to possess is the subject's inner, moral strength. The person portrayed is stoical towards everything, even towards aging and death. The sculptor seems to have transposed into the language of figurative art the words of Marcus Aurelius: "Either I will vanish altogether upon death, or I will be better off, but only provided I live rationally, performing my duties, and observing the laws of God."

ROMAN ART
Head of a Young Woman
Second half of 2nd century A.D.
Marble; height 10 5/8″
(This head of a young woman belonged to a life-size statue probably standing in a niche erected on a tomb. Found in Stolin, the ancient Salona).
Zagreb, Archaeological Museum

ROMAN PROVINCIAL ART
Tombstone of the Ennians
Middle of 2nd century A.D.
Marble from Pohorje; height 21′8″
(This monumental tombstone with rich relief decoration was discovered near Sempeter, Slovenia, in a necropolis of Romanized Celtic nobility).
Sempeter near Celje

ROMAN PROVINCIAL ART. *Tombstone of the Ennians.* *p. 47*

On the road between Emona (present-day Ljubljano) and Celeia (Celje), in the southwestern part of the Roman province of Noricum, near the modern village of Šempeter, a small necropolis of Romanized Celtic nobility was excavated between 1952 and 1955. At the end of the main alley of the ancient cemetery, this monumental tombstone was discovered, consisting of a plinth supporting a shrine containing the ashes of the deceased, and an edicula with canopy in which are portraits of the Ennian family. The basic form of this tomb is directly related to similar monuments in neighboring Italy, especially Etruria, dating from the Republican period. To this Italic scheme only the intermediate friezes and the architectural frames have been added, apparently imitated from a larger group of provincial steles in Pannonia and Noricum.

In spite of its artificial themes and classicist figurative solutions well known from 2nd century Roman art, the decoration of this tombstone as a whole has a special distinction. The upper part of the monument—the edicula—represents the world of the living, surmounted by the vault of the sky, while the relief decoration of the ash-shrine refers to the world of the dead. Quite unexpectedly, the edicula is pervaded by a somber atmosphere: at the upper right, Liberalis, the father of the family, is shown proudly holding his document of Roman citizenship in his left hand, though his consort Oppidana at left has not yet renounced her ancient Celtic costume, while below their daughter Calendina, oblivious of the two genii presaging her early death, is seen pretentiously wearing a hairdress in the fashion of the empress Faustina the Elder. In the decorative borders above, the hippocampi and the wreath, the lion chasing a horse and the dog pursuing a gazelle eloquently bespeak the forces that waylay everything noble and everything living, and witness the transitoriness and vanity of earthly life. On the lower part of the monument, the ash-shrine, everything is different, illuminated by a full light and bathed in undisturbed beauty: over the surface of the sea broken by a playful dolphin, Jupiter in the form of a bull is swiftly carrying Europa to the island of Crete (front), a nymph is playing with a satyr (left flank), and an eagle holding Ganymede is ascending towards Mount Olympus (right flank). These mythological themes are all allusions to life beyond the grave: the fulfillment of all desires (satyr and nymph), the voyage to the Blessed Isle (Europa on the bull), and the approach to the eternal gods (eagle with Ganymede). Unambiguously, on the *Tombstone of the Ennians* death is shown as a redemption and the greatest of all values.

ROMAN ART. *Mask from a Parade Helmet.* *p. 49*

This bronze mask with the face of a young man was originally part of a parade helmet typical of Roman ceremonial armor, which the foremost legionaires from the 1st to the 4th centuries wore in triumphal processions or with which they were interred in their tombs. It is not a realistic portrait giving a faithful representation of the individual's features, but an idealized face, an image of the abstract ideas of virility, human power and courage. This *Mask* (the ancient Vinceia), presents the features of a very young man, with his hair carefully arranged, a tense face without wrinkles, thin, arching eyebrows, elongated eyes, a long nose and sensual lips. To infuse this classically perfectioned, noble and soft face with the necessary vigor, the artist drew geometrically harsh contours, stressed the chin and sharply modelled the lines of eyebrows and nose. By this procedure, he combined in a single physiognomy the noble virility

48

ROMAN PROVINCIAL ART
Tombstones
Beginning of 4th century
Limestone; dimensions 37 1/2″ x 40 1/8″ and
24 3/4″ x 36 5/8″
(Parts of two tombstones representing the portraits of the deceased and a genre scene—horse and grooms. Found near Zenica, Bosnia, on the site of the Roman settlement of Bistua Nova).
Sarajevo, Regional Museum

which characterize the portraits of Emperor Hadrian with the type of beauty found in the numerous statues of his favorite Antinoüs, expressing the self-sacrificing bravery of a Roman legionary.

ROMAN PROVINCIAL ART. *Tombstones.* p. 50

These steles from Zenica follow a stereotyped Roman form, but they frankly feature the simple physiognomies of native personages and their local costume with pretentiously arranged folds and showy jewellery. The stone-cutting is far from remarkable: the relief is distinctly shallow, and the surfaces are rectangularly broken like in wood-carving, casting deep shadows over the surface. The figures are modelled without any sense of the third dimension, and are rather awkwardly arranged in space. But the quaint proportions and the pervading hesitation between naturalistic and decorative presentation give a peculiar charm to these monuments: an intimate atmosphere about these embraced figures seems to hover, full of pure, naïve poetry.

The almost brutal simplicity of the modelling, the insistence on symmetry and decorative value, the strong emphasis on certain traits of the face, and the outright contrast of light and shade on all the surfaces—these features are not elements of Roman art, but rather the essential characteristics of the Illyrian-Celtic style. The strong resemblance that the tombstones from Zenica also bear to the earliest pre-Romanesque sculptures indicates that this indigenous style of the Balkans and Central Europe was destined to survive Roman culture, and exert a decisive influence on the formation of European medieval sculpture.

LATE ANTIQUE ART
Communion of Mithra's Believers
Beginning of 4th century A.D.
Limestone; 23 1/4″ x 32 1/4″
(The ritual stone with scenes of Mithra killing a bull (front), and Mithra's believers communing (back) comes from a mithraeum discovered near Konjic).
Sarajevo, Regional Museum

LATE ANTIQUE ART
Hunters
About 300 A.D.
(Detail from a floor mosaic discovered in Gamzigrad, Eastern Serbia, in the sumptuous residence of an eminent courtier from the time of the First Tetrarchy).
Belgrade, Museum of 7 July

LATE ANTIQUE ART. *Communion of Mithra's Believers.* *p. 51*

The *Communion of Mithra's Believers* represented on this relief from Konjic indicates both by its iconography and by its style that by the beginning of the 4th century the mood of the pagan empire had turned towards universal concepts and towards gods whose cults implied rituals connected with abstract ideas and symbols. The task of the artist was to illustrate the steps of consecration, the hierarchy of believers in the god Mithra, and the communion by water and bread that assured salvation, immortality of the soul and resurrection. The loaves of bread marked with the sign of the cross on a small, round three-legged table, the gestures of the figures seated at a table covered with a sheep's skin, and the masks on the faces of the believers are the only essential elements of the scene; everything else is conventional accessory, for the attention of the observer must be restricted to the main content, to the one mystic idea, which has no need to be explained by convincing movements or realistic details.

LATE ANTIQUE ART. *Hunters.* *p. 52*

This floor mosaic from the palace of a Roman dignitary at Gamzigrad ranks among the outstanding monuments of late antique mosaic, and can well compete with the most beautiful mosaics of Sicily (Piazza Armerina), Constantinople (Imperial Palace) and Antiochia (Villa Daphne). It is adapted to the space of a large rectangular hall with a shallow nave along its axis, which dictated a tripartite division of the floor surface into a large central frieze and two flanking bands. These bands, decorated almost exclusively with geometrical motifs, only serve to emphasize the figurative decoration of the central frieze, which is divided into decorative compartments with scenes of combats between hunters and wild beasts. The pictorial effects are dramatic. By means of varicolored, richly nuanced mosaic stones, the most subtle transitions and shades of color are rendered, and there is a continuity of contour and movement. The figures of the hunters are unnaturally elongated, and their handsome, dignified faces show no traces of effort or fear. A large round shield in the foreground is set to indicate depth; but the background, which is completely empty, like an opaque curtain or a monochrome setting, has a powerful effect.

EARLY CHRISTIAN ART. *Garden of Paradise.* *p. 54*

The floor mosaic from the narthex of the large basilica of Heraclea eloquently illustrates how early Christian art, with its limited, chiefly traditional means, nevertheless succeeded in expressing quite novel ideas on the structure of the universe and the human soul.

The composition of the mosaic is very simple. A narrow border, with 36 octagonal fields representing the fish of the sea, frames a large frieze showing animals in the Garden of Paradise, while the center of the frieze is occupied by a medallion featuring a cantharus vessel and a vine, flanked by peacocks and deer. Not a single theme of this mosaic is new: the composition within the medallion is related to the ancient heraldic formulas of Mesopotamia and Crete, the garden with the fruit trees is a lively reminder of the gardens of the Phaeacian king Alcinoüs and the landscapes represented in the frescoes of the Casa Livia in Rome, while the animals themselves are modelled on those appearing in Sassanian or Antiochian art. As to the iconographic significance, the images

EARLY CHRISTIAN ART
Garden of Paradise
End of 5th century A.D.
Central frieze of a mosaic, 63' 8" × 8'6"
(Detail of a floor mosaic discovered in the ruins of Heraclea near Bitola, Macedonia, in the narthex of a large basilica. A cedar tree, surrounded by flying birds, is flanked by a wild goat, and by rosebushes, lilies and ivy).
Bitola, Museum of Heraclea

contained within the border (animals dwelling in the water), the frieze (wild beasts and fruit-trees, with flocks of birds flying around them) and the central medallion (cantharus and vine) clearly represent the four domains of the universe—the Ocean, Earth, Sky, and the sphere of the sensually inaccessible. The mosaic from Heraclea, however, is not intended merely to illustrate the structure of the universe in a scientific, astronomical, religious, or literary sense; primarily it purports to represent and evaluate the various stages of the human soul at a painful moment of transition from one historical and psychological situation to another, new one. The theme of the border is not just a schematic picture of the Ocean surrounding the Earth; rather, it symbolizes primitive water, its forbidding darkness, and all the forces lurking in the depths of the subconscious, while the trees of the Earth signify the integral man.

LATE ANTIQUE ART. *Roman Emperor.*

This *Portrait of a Roman Emperor,* probably representing Valens, marks the synthesis of Graeco-Roman and Oriental esthetics. The head is modelled in the fashion of the East, simply, with summary traits and large surfaces, with no attempt at realism and deprived of all unessential details. But in contrast to the unattractive, awkward faces from the period between 195 and 325, this portrait from Niš is distinguished by a certain softness, and is to some extent even a life-like resemblance. But it is no more the realism of ancient Graeco-Roman art, flightingly revived in the reign of Constantine I, upon the fortunate conclusion of civil wars and the promulgation of the edict of Milan. Actually, the emperor's head obeys a figurative scheme hitherto unknown, in which neither in-

LATE ANTIQUE ART
Roman Emperor (Valens?)
Between 360 and 380 A.D.
Hollow cast bronze with traces of gilding; height 14 1/8″
(Portrait of a Roman emperor found in Niš, the ancient Naissus).
Belgrade, National Museum

55

dividual psychological and physical traits of the personality are portrayed, nor any agitated lines and surfaces, nor anything changeable and transitory is admitted. The lips are compressed, the lower part of the face looks empty, the ears seem unnaturally large, and the forehead is contracted in height and extended in width, to lay a more forceful emphasis on the eyes, the stare and something concentrated in a point above the juncture of the arched brows. The form thus modelled addresses the irrational functions of consciousness.

ART OF THE MIGRATION PERIOD. *Arched Fibula.*
Within the walls of Ulpiana—a large Roman and Byzantine city—a solitary Germanic tomb has been discovered, containing an exceptionally rich treasure. The large arched fibula from this grave, a product of the Pannonian jewellery workshops catering chiefly to the Lombards, is stylistically articulated: everything is stylized along the surface plane, zoömorphic and vegetable motifs are presented in organic conjunction with geometrical ornaments, and the main stress is laid on optical, coloristic effects. Estheticians like Worringer and Riegl have confronted the clear morphology of this surface-bound ornamental style to the amorphousness of three-dimensional, organically modelled forms, and pointed out its rationality and beauty.

LATE ANTIQUE ART. *Cameo of a Victorious Emperor.* p. 57
In contrast to the tranquil figures of rulers featured on the official cameos of the Hellenistic and early Roman imperial periods, this late antique *Cameo* from Kusatak represents the emperor on a prancing horse, trampling on conquered barbarians. This altered iconography reflects the profound transformations of the ancient world at the beginning of the 4th century, and suggests an atmosphere quite unknown to earlier times, apparently still glorious and joyful, but in essence haunted by convulsions and perplexities.

In the lower part of the cameo, like a modern comic strip, the figures of the defeated, killed or dominated enemies are laid out in a row. The emperor is triumphant, but his swinging right hand holding a spear and his prancing horse clearly indicate that he cannot yet afford to rest, and that final victory can hardly be envisaged. The spear and the horse are directed towards something facing them which is not represented in the picture. The space beyond the emperor is evidently not empty, for the horse, though represented in headlong plunge, seems at the same time to be shuddering back from some insurmountable obstacle, while the outstretched right hand holding the spear seems congealed by some terrifying force. This can only be the new, fresh force of the barbarian troops that continued to flood the northern frontiers of the empire throughout the 4th century, in spite of the victories of Constantine I and his successors.

LATE ANTIQUE ART. *Parade Helmet.* p. 58
The limits of the Roman empire fixed along the right bank of the Danube for a long time firmly separated the ancient from the barbarian world, or rather the Mediterranean civilization from the still prehistoric cultures of Central Europe. From year to year, from decade to decade the hostility between these two irreconcilable worlds continued to increase, and after the second half of the 3rd century the Danube basin became a huge battlefield.

This precious *Parade Helmet* from Berkasovo is probably a prize of war hidden

ART OF THE MIGRATION PERIOD
Arched Fibula
Middle of 6th century A.D.
Cast silver, gilt; length 4 7/8"
Prishtina, Museum of Kosovo and Metohija

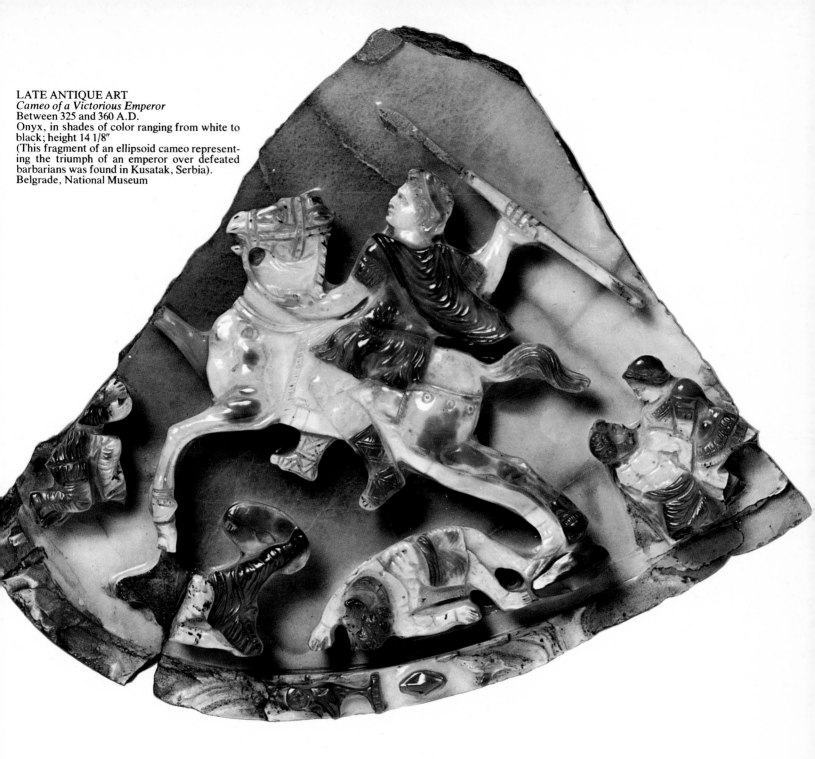

LATE ANTIQUE ART
Cameo of a Victorious Emperor
Between 325 and 360 A.D.
Onyx, in shades of color ranging from white to black; height 14 1/8″
(This fragment of an ellipsoid cameo representing the triumph of an emperor over defeated barbarians was found in Kusatak, Serbia).
Belgrade, National Museum

underground after an indecisive battle. Its maker, Avitus, and its owner Dizon were undoubtedly subjects of the empire, possibly even christianized, but their taste is barbarian and their religious beliefs evidently filled with superstition. The helmet is profusely decorated with geometrical motifs characteristic of Germanic and Gepidian art objects. The technique of overlaying with gilt plate and insetting with varicolored stones is another feature of barbarian art. Three kinds of precious stones are imitated by glass paste: emerald (in the rectangular sockets), onyx (in the oval sockets) and blue chalcedon (in the round sockets). Their apotropaic powers were widely believed not only by the barbarians, but also by the lower strata of Roman society.

p. 58
LATE ANTIQUE ART
Parade Helmet
About 320 A.D.
Height 13 3/4″
(The helmet consists of calotte with crest, frontal ring, check pieces and neck plate. A 1/8″ base of forged steel is covered with a 1/16″ layer of gilt silver plate decorated with geometric ornaments in relief, insets of multicolored glass paste, and rivets fitted with globules of silver. The two bands attached to the frontal ring bear a Greek inscription indicating that the helmet was made by Avitus and intended for a man named Dizon. The helmet was found in 1955 in Berkasovo, Vojvodina).
Novi Sad, Museum of Vojvodina

PART III
MIDDLE AGES
(Imaginary Figures and Spaces)

ROMANESQUE ART. *Diptych.* *The Virgin with Christ Enthroned*
This *Diptych* from the Strossmayer Gallery, like most ivory carvings of the early Middle Ages, is eclectic in style. The frontally represented figures of the Virgin and Christ, with their unflattering, realistically modelled faces, are based on examples of Carolingian art (ivories of the Adda group), which were in themselves not original, but in turn dependent on similar early Christian compositions from the end of the 5th and the first half of the 6th centuries. This traditional figurative scheme is, however, expressed with a monumentality and sense of decoration unknown in earlier times: the massive figures with their strongly modelled heads are contrasted with the complicated, linearly rendered folds of the draperies. These are characteristics of Western European art from the period of the Saxon emperors, above all typical of the workshops of the imperial Benedictine Abbey of Reichenau.

ROMANESQUE ART
Diptych: The Virgin with Christ Enthroned
Between 972 and 976
Carved ivory book cover; 9″ x 4″
Zagreb, Strossmayer Gallery

ROMANESQUE ART
Crucifix
Bronze with blue enamel; 8 1/2″ x 4 3/4″
(This cross of processional type is decorated with rosettes, and at its base with the stylized images of the top of Mount Calvary. Christ is represented with a crown on his head and a peplum around his thighs).
Parish church of Lokve near Divača, Slovenia

ROMANESQUE ART. *Crucifix.* *p. 61*
The portal of St. Trophime Church, Arles, and the façade of Angoulème Cathedral had certainly been built by the time this bronze and enamel *Crucifix* from Lokve near Divaca was rendered by an unknown master—probably a member of the enamel workshops of Limoges.

This is not an image of a dead god nailed to the cross, nor an illustration of the story of his sufferings. Christ here is alive, his eyes are penetrating, all the muscles of his body tense, and his hands vigorously outstretched; he is part of the cross itself, and at the same time represented both as a divine king and as a man willing to accept all mankind and all the universe in his embrace. The cross is not merely the image of the tree on Mount Golgotha, but a symbol of man and his fate. Into that primeval concept—which in prehistoric cults symbolized the rays of the sun; in Indian religions the co-ordinates of the universe; and in Cretan belief the omnipotence of the Great Goddess—only Christianity introduced man as the highest value of all. The miraculous, liberating and pacifying significance of the cross in the European world is based precisely on its new, humanist content.

PRE-ROMANESQUE SCULPTURE
Scenes from the Life of Christ
End of 11th century; 38 1/2″ x 92 1/2″
Stone plaque (*pluteus*) with reliefs representing
scenes from the Gospels (from Annunciation to
Adoration of the Magi)
From the destroyed Sveta Nedelja Church, Za-
dar.
Zadar, Archaeological Museum

PRE-ROMANESQUE SCULPTURE.   *Scenes from the Life of Christ.*
This relief from the destroyed church of Sveta Nedelja, Zadar, shows that even
the representation of human figures and iconographically complicated themes
from the Gospels do not essentially affect the basic ornamental style of pre-
Romanesque sculpture. Foreign influences, in particular those from Asia Minor
and from Coptic art, are clearly visible. On the frescoes of Cappadocian
churches scenes from Christ's life are narrated in a way similar to this plaque
from Sveta Nedelja Church, while an identical arrangement of figures appears in
an ivory relief carving that probably originated in the circle of Coptic or Syrian
art. We must, however, not over-emphasize the importance of these Near Eastern sources when evaluating pre-Romanesque sculpture. Coptic art—and Near
Eastern art in general—cherishes a decorative style in which even figurative subjects are decomposed into arabesques. Pre-Romanesque sculpture, which is also
basically ornamental, therefore accepts without resistance this figurativeness
dissolved into two-dimensionality, easily blends it with its own elements of inter-
weaving ornament, and develops it as if it were its own creation.

PRE-ROMANESQUE SCULPTURE.   *Plaque from Split Baptistery.*   p. 63
The paths along which European medieval sculpture originated are rather intricate and obscure. By stressing its antique traditions, its Near Eastern and Byzantine influences or the contributions of the creative forces of the Lombards
or even the newly settled Slavs, it is impossible to explain wholly the specific
style of pre-Romanesque sculpture that developed from the 8th to the 12th

PRE-ROMANESQUE SCULPTURE
Plaque from Split Baptistery
Second half of 11th century
Stone; 41" x 25 1/2" x 4 3/4"
Probably part of an altar screen (*pluteus*).
Split, Baptistery of the Cathedral

centuries along the Adriatic coasts, in Central and Northern Italy, the Alpine regions, France and Southern Spain. Irrespective of their considerable differences in ethnic, social and economic structure, all these classic regions of pre-Romanesque sculpture share a common heritage of Roman culture in the recent past, and Celtic culture in the more distant past. Therefore one can presume that the medieval sculpture of Western Europe arose from a revival of the traditional Celtic style, which after the decay of the Western Roman Empire easily blended with the ornamental motifs of late antique art. Only in the course of the further development of the style, this base was transformed by local forces, as well as by the influences of the art of Byzantium, the Copts or Asia Minor.

This *Plaque from the Baptistery of Split* belongs to the developed, classic pre-Romanesque style. It is difficult to define the precise time when the relief was carved. Pre-Romanesque sculpture developed within the framework of the Croatian medieval state into a style of imaginative and effective wavy decoration, in which the human figure only began to appear in later times—probably after the middle of the 11th century. The country's prosperity under the kings Petar Krešimir and Dimitrije Zvonimir was no doubt decisive in the choice of the subject. The crowned personage on the throne—with a figure on his right standing in glory, and a second figure prostrate on the ground—clearly stresses both the power of the celestial ruler and the glory of the earthly; it is addressed both to the members of the Christian church and to the king's subjects.

MEDIEVAL CHURCH EMBROIDERY. *Epitrachelion.*

Beneath the central medallion showing the figure of Christ—to a large extent destroyed—a group of saints is embroidered in silk. They are placed under arcades and arranged in three superimposed rows: the Virgin Mary and John the Baptist in praying attitude (central composition of the Deisis), and two rows of Fathers of the Church, who are shown with books in their left hands (St. John Chrysostome and St. Basil the Great; St. Gregory the Theologian and St. Nicholas). The capitals of the arcade columns (with interlacing motifs) as well as the ornament of the rectangular fields (tendrils, crosses in embroidered medallions, stylized palmettes and birds, continuous interlace) are related to the decorative sculpture of the Morava school, indicating that this example of sumptuous church embroidery was produced within the borders of the Serbian state at the end of the 14th or in the first years of the 15th century.

MEDIEVAL CHURCH EMBROIDERY
Epitrachelion (stole, detail)
End of 14th to beginning of the 15th century
Silk, embroidered with silver and varicolored
silk thread; 59" x 9 7/8"
(This epitrachelion was found in the tomb of the
Metropolitan of Raška in St. Peter's Church
near Novi Pazar, Serbia).
Belgrade, National Museum

BYZANTINE ART OF THE ELEVENTH
CENTURY
Archangel
Second quarter of the 11th century
(This archangel is a part of the *Ascension*, a
huge fresco painted in the time of archbishop
Leo on the altar ceiling of the Cathedral Church
of St. Sophia, Ochrid).
Ochrid, St. Sophia Church
Belgrade, Fresco Gallery (copy)

BYZANTINE ART OF THE ELEVENTH CENTURY. *Archangel.* p. 65

The frescoes surrounding the altar of St. Sophia Church, Ochrid, represent both the culmination of the Byzantine renascence during the Macedonian dynasty, and foreshadow the dignified, serious, classically medieval style of the period of the Comnenes.

This *Archangel* stands quietly and majestically among the figures of the excited apostles, who follow Christ's Ascension to heaven with upturned heads and lively gestures. The Archangel is the only figure in the whole composition turned towards the believers; and it is to them that the penetrating gaze and authoritative gesture of the right hand pointing at the Ascension—a manifestation of God's omnipotence—are addressed. The Archangel's head is powerfully painted. The sweeping contour of the chin, the complicated drawing around the eyes, the wrinkle separating the eyebrows and the small, compressed lids take all human warmth from this figure, partly deform it, and endow it with one passion only—the ruthless plea for Christian belief.

The painter of this representation of the *Ascension* is unknown. It is difficult today to define precisely what are the sources for his visionary, expressionistic style. The great cycles of Byzantine painting of the 9th and 10th centuries have not been preserved, while the known monuments from the first half of the 11th century (the mosaics from the churches of Nea Moni, Chios, of St. Luke, Phokis, and of St. Sophia, Kiev) are only formally close to the style of the Ochrid *Ascension*. The plastic definition of the figures of this monumental composition no doubt owes a great deal to the classicist style of 10th century miniatures, but the cool color, the expressiveness and the intense spirituality seem to be adopted from much older monuments of early Christian art. This archaism is not accidental, but reflects the authority of the Byzantine state and church.

PAINTER OF NEREZI
Birth of the Virgin Mary
1164
(Fresco in the naos of St. Panteleimon Church).
Nerezi near Skopolje, St. Panteleimon Church
Belgrade, Fresco Gallery (copy)

PAINTER OF NEREZI. *Birth of the Virgin Mary.*

The scenes from the life of the Virgin Mary in the church of Nerezi—in particular the fresco representing the *Birth of Mary*—rank among the liveliest and most realistic creations of 12th century Byzantine art. Within a sumptuous architectonic frame, in a space suffused with light, the figures are arranged in a balanced way into three groups, each of which communicates its own rhythm.

In the center of the composition St. Ann, half reclining, is flanked by two figures who sustain her with careful attention. To the left and right of this quiet and solemn central group, busy, diligent women fill the scene; it is to them that the divine child is entrusted; they carry the water and scents for her bath, and show by their movements, both animated and dignified, that they are aware of the greatness of the moment and the importance of the event in which they are taking part. The bright palette, in which pure tones of brown and ochre predominate, the warm tapestries and the richly decorated draperies introduce into the scene a worldly atmosphere of court luxury and informal serenity.

GREGORY THE DEACON. *Initial from the Miroslav Gospel.*

As in the first documents of Serbian monumental art (the earliest sequence of frescoes in St. Peter's Church, Ras), western Romanesque elements are predominant in the miniatures of the *Miroslav Gospel.* These are apparent both in the technique of illumination (pen-drawing, partly filled in with color), in their form (emphasis on initials, as opposed to chapter headings, and choice of color) and in their content (choice of themes, composition). Only a small part of the nearly three hundred very large initials with human and animal figures interwoven within a lacework of plant forms show elements clearly adopted from Byzantine, Syrian or Coptic illuminated manuscripts. One of these is the initial on page 115, which adheres to the Romanesque style only by its size and patterns, while its composition (confronted birds carrying palmettes in their bills) is linked, through the early Christian ornament of the 6th century, to models from Eastern, Sassanian art.

GREGORY THE DEACON (BIJAK GLIGO-RIJE)
Initial from the Miroslav Gospel Book
Ca. 1180–1190
Pen and watercolor on parchment; height of initial 3 3/4″
(Initial "P" on page 115 of the Gospel Book belonging to Miroslav Duke of Hum, the earliest preserved Serbian Cyrillic manuscript on parchment; page 16 1/2″ x 11 1/4″
Belgrade, National Museum

PAINTER OF NEREZI. *St. Panteleimon.* p. 68

The new sensibility which, upon the ascent of the Comnene dynasty, breaks the hard shell of the hieratic forms of Byzantine art, is magnificently exemplified in the frescoes of St. Panteleimon Church, Nerezi.

The marble iconostasis frames the figure of the patron saint of the church: fashionably elongated, rendered in restrained movement, with a gracile head and calligraphically elaborated details. The folds of the draperies are represented with stressed linearism, echoing that of the 11th century monuments; but the expression of the saint's face is no longer severe, merely abstaining from all human desires, intentions and activities. St. Panteleimon's head, in spite of its obvious stylization (the thin neck, the sharp outline of the chin, the unnaturally enlarged eyes), creates rather the effect of an idealized portrait of a noble courtier than the image of an abstractly conceived saint. The figure is only formally conventional, in its outside appearance and its pose, while a new, hitherto unknown personal note has been introduced—an indication of intellectual curiosity, of the right to think more freely about people and life.

PAINTER OF NEREZI. *Lamentation over the Body of Christ.* p. 70–71

It has often been pointed out that the unknown painter of the *Lamentation* in the church of Nerezi was a whole century ahead of the normal current of European medieval art: he was the first to introduce realism in Byzantine painting, and thus foreshadowed the achievements of Italian Renaissance much earlier than Giotto. In its drama and expressive power the Nerezi *Lamentation* is, in fact, close to Giotto's fresco of the same theme, the Pietà from the Scrovegna Chapel, Padua; nevertheless, these two masterpieces of medieval art are separated by a profound, unbridgeable abyss.

During his whole life Giotto di Bondone cherished a love for nature, its open spaces, plastic forms and bright, pure colors. The sensibility of the unknown painter of the Nerezi *Lamentation* was formed in a different environment, under the shadow of a capital city, court and church, under the influence of liturgical texts and apocryphal literature. Therefore the greatest of all human pains—the lament of a mother over the body of her dead son—is expressed in the church of Nerezi in an esthetic manner entirely different from that of the Scrovegna Chapel: not by rational, plastic forms and strident colors, but by irrational lines and subdued tones.

The *Lamentation over the Body of Christ* subsists on its graphic qualities, broad contours and a profusion of thin lines indicating the details, but limited in colors and tones. The greens, browns, ochres and whites are blended with the predominant blue into quiet, sad color harmonies, recalling the chant of funeral liturgy, thus giving a sense to death and mitigating the drama of the scene. There is no plastic balance in the composition. The Virgin embracing Christ's cold and lifeless body in an almost prostrate position is set off-center. From her, the axis of the painting leads back to the lowly bending figure of St. John, to St. Joseph and St. Nicodemus kneeling behind him, and to the bearer of spices standing at the further end. From Christ's head, the composition visually expands over the heads of the Virgin and St. John towards that of the spice bearer; emotionally, it descends along the same line: where the mass is most reduced, the pain is most intense. By this procedure the entire composition is a toppled pyramid, whose overthrown peak comprises the essential feature.

PAINTER OF NEREZI
St. Panteleimon
1164
(This marble iconostatis with stucco decoration on its arch and the icon of St. Panteleimon in fresco, belongs to the church of Nerezi erected by the Byzantine prince Alexis the Angel).
Nerezi near Skopolje, St. Panteleimon Church
Belgrade, Fresco Gallery (copy)

p. 70–71
PAINTER OF NEREZI
Lamentation over the Body of Christ
1164
Fresco in the naos of St. Panteleimon Church.
Nerezi near Skopolje, St. Panteleimon Church
Belgrade, Fresco Gallery (copy)

PAINTER OF MILEŠEVO
Angel at the Tomb of Christ
About 1235
(This angel is a detail of *Spice Bearers at the Tomb of Christ*, painted in the naos of the Church of the Ascension erected in Milesevo by King Vladislav).
Milesevo near Prijepolje, Serbia, Church of the Ascension
Belgrade, Fresco Gallery (copy)

PAINTER OF MILEŠEVO
Ca. 1235
Portrait of the Founder
(The south wall of the west transept of the Church of the Ascension includes a portrait of King Vladislav, preceded by the Virgin Mary and offering a model of the church to Christ).
Mileševo near Prijepolje, Serbia, Church of the Ascension
Belgrade, Fresco Gallery (copy)

PAINTER OF MILEŠEVO.   *Angel at the Tomb of Christ.*   *p. 72*

In the development of Serbian medieval painting, the frescoes in the naos of the Church of the Ascension, Mileševo, mark the crucial moment of finding and consolidating an original, national style of expression, while in the context of European art they stand out as one of the first clear foreshadowings of the Renaissance spirit. All that was best in the contemporary output of Constantinople (refined forms), Thessalonika (mastery of drawing) and Italy (lyricism and color contrast) is found in the decoration of Milesevo Church, happily combined and instilled with new forces sprung up within the frontiers of the independent Serbian state.

The importance and splendor of the court are reflected in the great number of secular portraits, while the freer intellectual currents are expressed in the quite unusual arrangement of the sacred compositions. Among these, the representation of *Spice Bearers at the Tomb of Christ,* with its monumental figure of a seated angel, is a major masterpiece. The delicate blue, golden and white coloring illuminate the figure with a light that belongs to this world, while the warm tones of the flesh and the plastic elaboration of the draperies create lifelike volumes, intersecting in mild half-tones. The *Angel*'s pose with pointing gesture is dignified and kingly; while his face expresses an intimate, lyrical mood. This figure is not presented in the manner of any medieval style, nor in the spirit of antiquity. It is the product of a new, cosmopolitan art.

PAINTER OF MILEŠEVO. *Portrait of the Founder.* p. 73

The portrait of the founder, King Vladislav, appears at the western end of Mileševo church; it shows the king, preceded by the Virgin Mary, presenting a
model of his church to Christ. The head of the young king is elaborated with
graphic detail reminiscent of the technique of icon-painting, but is illuminated
by the lively color of monumental fresco-painting. The rounded outlines and
the yellow, white and ochre flesh tones give a compulsive reality to the figure,
while carefully observed details—the tender, newly grown beard, the wrinkles
around the eyes, the drooping cheeks—emphasize intellectual preoccupations
and moods. The large blue eyes do not seem to belong to this incongruously
broad, fleshy head. But it is precisely this contrast that attracts our attention to
the expression of those eyes, which seem both reproachful and filled with tenderness, and at the same time expressing the tragic recognition that man can
never express his deepest thoughts and that inevitably a large part of his love,
goodness and finest words die with him unexpressed. The painter of this portrait can be ranked among the first "intimists" in European art.

PAINTER OF THE CHURCH OF THE MOTHER OF GOD,
STUDENICA. *Fathers of the Church.* p. 75

Contemporary with the decay of the Byzantine empire in the period between
the death of Manuel Comnene (1180) and the fall of Constantinople (1204), the
continental regions of the Balkans saw the rapid growth of the young Serbian
state and the astonishing expansion of its original and fresh court art.

The earliest frescoes of the Church of the Mother of God at Studenica, though
the work of Greek artists, differ considerably from the decorative linearism of
Comnene painting. With their peculiar style, severe and archaic in appearance,
they formulate the basic standpoints of Serbian medieval art. The paintings
surrounding the altar represent liturgical themes on a yellow background: the
monumental figure of the Virgin , beneath it the *Communion of the Apostles
and Archpriests.* The lowest zone of this famous altar apse shows the *Fathers
of the Church.* The figures of these venerable sages of the orthodox church are
rendered on a monumental scale, in rigid poses, with forceful brush-strokes
and sober color. Their huge bodies with unnaturally thin, small hands and impressive heads with high, intelligent foreheads, seem to be modelled on earlier
achievements of festive mosaic art. The figures of St. Gregory and St. Cyril are
physically individualized, but they both seem to be driven by the same inner
preoccupations. They seem to convey the same questions and messages that
St. Sava, first abbot of Studenica, addressed to the brotherhood of this church:
"How terrifying will Christ's face be . . . will he accept us among the right-
eous in the Kingdom of Heaven, or send us to eternal pain among the sinners?"

PAINTER OF SOPOĆANI. *Assumption of the Virgin Mary.* p. 76, 77

At a time when Cimabue and Niccolò Pisano in Italy were striving to liberate
form from hieratic rigidity, and when the Byzantine court, preoccupied with
the restoration of the empire and harassed by financial crisis, was renouncing
all major artistic projects, in the economically powerful Serbian state of Uroš I
the large fresco of the *Assumption of the Virgin* was painted on the west wall of

74

the naos of Sopoćani Church. This monumental composition boldly breaks the framework of medieval esthetics, and in a new space and in a new brilliant light stresses the long forgotten beauty of the total human personality.

The huge surface of this fresco (20'8" × 14') is flooded with human figures. The composition is nevertheless organized with the utmost clarity, for all the masses are carefully organized into six groups, six pyramidal volumes of varying heights and structures, which are skillfully disposed on three different planes. The central pyramid, containing the Virgin lying on a platform at its base and the standing figure of Christ at its axis, is flanked by the groups of apostles, set in the foreground but on a slightly lower level. In the background, forming the third plane of the picture, is the high pyramid consisting of bishops and angels, framed by architectural elements painted in inverse perspective. The broad, fluent lines of the drawing and the surfaces colored in contrasting tones give each figure the appearance of a colossal statue, while the diverse gestures of the figures in the first plane open a clear view to those set behind them in depth. Though each group is moved by its own rhythm and emotional expression, they are all subordinated to the main protagonists shown in the center. Therefore the entire composition has the effect of an enormous, well-harmonized polyphonic choir, heroically sonorous with epic solemnity. The bright harmonies of red-green and violet-green harmonize through the slightly darker tones of the third plane into the golden background, the radiant luminosity of the sky, from where Christ is descending with his angels and apostles. By this procedure the painter of Sopoćani realized the radiance for which his contemporary Domentian yearned—"the light that we will only see with the angels, that has no beginning and no end." The artist's brush was simultaneously able to model volumes with concentrated spiritual and physical force.

PAINTER OF SOPOĆANI
Assumption of the Virgin Mary
Ca. 1265
(Fresco on the west wall of the naos of Church of the Trinity, founded in Sopoćani by King Uroš I).
Sopoćani near Novi Pazar, Serbia, Church of the Trinity
Belgrade, Fresco Gallery (copy)

PAINTER OF SOPOĆANI
Assumption of the Virgin Mary
Detail

76

PAINTER OF THE KING'S CHURCH, STUDENICA.   *Introduction to the Temple.*

The frescoes of the King's Church, Studenica, were created in the finest traditions of Byzantine art. Their small size, their iconography and their "zoögraphic", lifelike style are strongly reminiscent of the much earlier miniature painting of the 10th and 11th centuries. This scene of the *Introduction to the Temple* avoids almost all the weaknesses of the paintings of the Paleologue renaissance—the complicated content, obtrusive story-telling, routine drawing—yet preserves and emphasizes its qualities: the beauty of form, the poetical details, the deep space and the warmth of color. The artist was evidently acquainted with the recent production of Constantinople, but his work also demonstrates the presence of a local tradition, with reminiscences of the monumental court style of Mileševo and Sopoćani. The influence of this tradition is clearly apparent in the simplicity of content and the calm, logical compositional scheme. The decorative architecture in the background, the representation of unaffected gestures, and the colors increasingly muted as one proceeds from the foreground towards the background, give this scene of the *Introduction to the Temple* a classicist and theatrical total effect.

PAINTER OF ST. DEMETRIUS CHURCH, PEĆ
Girl with Amphora
Between 1338 and 1346
(Detail from the fresco representing *The Birth of the Virgin Mary* in the altar of St. Demetrius' Church, erected in Peć by archbishop Nicodemus between 1318 and 1324. In the altar apse, by the side of the figure of The Virgin Mary, the signature of the chief painter is inscribed in Greek: "Gift to God, from the hand of John").
Peć, St. Demetrius Church
Belgrade, Fresco Gallery (copy)

PAINTER OF ST. DEMETRIUS CHURCH, PEĆ. *Girl with Amphora.*
As a reaction to the classicist and representational court art, the decorations in the foundation of the Serbian archbishops executed after 1325 show a tendency to represent sacred themes in a simpler and stricter style.

The frescoes of St. Demetrius Church clearly express the ambitions of the high clergy immediately before the proclamation of the Serbian patriarchate in 1346. The *Girl with Amphora*, a detail from the scene of the *Birth of the Virgin Mary*, is probably a work of master John (Jovan), whose signature is preserved in the dome of the altar apsis. It is painted with dark, dense colors, among which the light tones stand out in strong contrast, mostly in the form of narrow, broken stripes. But though this contrast between light and dark is pronounced, it is rather lifeless and undramatic. The lighter surfaces are all geometricized and overwhelmed by the dominant tones of green, so the effect is that of a hermetically closed space, with figures that seem to be illuminated as if through a veil. This impression of unreality is even heightened by the elongated body of the girl, her unnaturally thin arms and ascetic physiognomy. Reminders of the earlier classicism are only perceptible in some details and requisites. Everything else—the abrupt movements, the cold narration, and the emphasis on a single plane—corresponds to the austere monastic spirit of Mount Athos.

79

ICON FROM OCHRID
St. Matthew the Evangelist
End of 13th century
Tempera painting on wood; 41 3/4" x 22 1/4"
Chief icon from the Church of St. Mary Peri-
bleptos
(St. Clement), at Ochrid.
Ochrid, Icon Gallery, Church of St. Clement

ICON FROM OCHRID
St. Matthew the Evangelist
80 Detail

ICON FROM OCHRID. *St. Matthew the Evangelist.* p. 80, 81

The majestic figure of *St. Matthew the Evangelist* dates from in the last years of the 13th century, immediately after the dissolution of the union between the Western and Eastern churches, at a time when Andronicus II was determined to strengthen monasticism and orthodoxy in Byzantium. This radical break in politics is clearly reflected in the artistic creations of the so-called Paleologue renaissance, which meant, on the one hand, a return to the ancient traditions, and on the other a strong affirmation of the ambitions of the restored Byzantine empire and the orthodox church.

This figure of *St. Matthew*, monumental in size and sculpturesque in treatment, is strongly reminiscent of the figures in the frescoes of the church of St. Mary Peribleptos in Ochrid, which are probably a creation of two painters from Thessalonika, Michael and Eutychio. The contours are sharp, the folds of the fluttering draperies all broken and illuminated with contrasting highlights, while the rendering of the flesh with ochre and deep strawberry colored shadows emphasizes the relief-like structure of the head and endows the figure with power. St. Matthew is depicted in motion, with his Gospel open in his hands; as there is not a single quiet line, nor a single larger surface without halftones, the distinctive character of the Evangelist is his bold impetuosity and over-emphasized ardor, which deprive the figure of any genuine monumentality and inner certainty. This dynamic, nervous style is a faithful reflection of the contemporary political situation: the strong, impatient desire to renew the former glory of Byzantium, in spite of the shattered economy and foreign pressures.

ICON FROM OCHRID. *Descent into Hell.* p. 82, left

This *Descent into Hell* shows the hand of a great master who, within the small size of the icon, realizes all the basic aspirations of the mature art of the Paleologues. The numerous figures surrounding Christ are arranged in three mutually balanced groups, but by skillfully linking the extended hands of Christ and Adam the painter stresses a single dominant diagonal in his composition, while everything else is relegated to shadow and to the second plane. This diagonal, strengthened by the pointed rocks in the right background and the white of Christ's vestments, appears like a strong beam of light projected into the depths of hell; it reinforces the dynamism of Christ's and Adam's gestures and emphasizes the contact of their hands as the main content of the painting.

ICON FROM OCHRID. *Crucifixion.* p. 82, right

It was probably Andronicus II Paleologue who presented this icon of the *Crucifixion*—painted in a Constantinople workshop in the first years of the 14th century—to archbishop Gregory of Ochrid. That emperor, though not too successful in his foreign policy, nevertheless restored peace to the world of Eastern Christianity, renewed the power of the patriarchate of Constantinople, and thus initiated a revival of church art. This icon from Ochrid is a witness of the new wealth and stability of the church, and its perfectionist, poised style is a reflection of the refined taste of the highly educated court aristocracy. The composition is simple and balanced, the drawing delicate, and the gestures dignified.

ICON FROM OCHRID
Descent into Hell
Beginning of 14th century
Tempera on wood; 18 1/4″ x 15 1/8″
Icon from the Church of St. Mary Peribleptos
(St. Clement) in Ochrid.
Ochrid, Icon Gallery, Church of St. Clement

ICON FROM OCHRID
Crucifixion
Beginning of 14th century
Tempera 37 1/4″ x 27 3/4″
Verso of a two-sided icon (the front side represents *Christ the Shepherd of Souls*), from the Church of St. Mary Peribleptos (St. Clement) in Ochrid.
Ochrid, Icon Gallery, Church of St. Clement

ICON FROM OCHRID
Annunciation
Beginning of 14th century
Tempera on wood; 37 1/4″ x 27 3/4″
Verso of a two-sided icon (the front side represents *St. Mary the Shepherdess of Souls*), from the Church of St. Mary Peribleptos (St. Clement) in Ochrid.
Ochrid, Icon Gallery, Church of St. Clement

ICON FROM OCHRID. *Annunciation.*   *p. 83*
To the painter of this great icon, the theme of the *Annunciation*—both deeply
spiritual and full of earthly joy—was an occasion to illustrate the virtues and
weaknesses of the art of the Paleologue renaissance. The artist skillfully balances the basic masses of the picture, draws his outlines lightly and unobtru-
sively, and splendidly composes his colors into two basic harmonies: purple-
green-crimson, and blue-grey-brown. Like the Sienese masters of a century later, he carefully models the delicate faces of the Virgin and the archangel Gabri-
el in light ochre, yellow and crimson. But he does not succeed in establishing
the intimate contact between the two figures implied by the solemn moment of
the *Annunciation*. In spite of the archangel's outstretched right hand and the
restrained gesture of the Virgin, the two actors of the scene remain mutually
isolated—they are set on pedestals of unequal height, and seem to be two separate entities artificially brought together. But this lack of intimacy, like the
overcrowding of the composition with architectural details, is richly compensated for by the high pictorial quality of the icon.

SERBIAN SECULAR EMBROIDERY. *Cloak of King Milutin.*   *p. 85*
On dark-red silk framed by velvet, the figure of the dead Christ, flanked by two
six-winged seraphim and six attendant angels, is embroidered with gold and silver thread, and silk thread of ochre, green, blue, violet and white. In spite of
the closed eyes, Christ's face is handsome and expressive, while his body, with
its pronounced anatomical details, is virile and strong. The angels are more
softly modelled, and the abundant folds of their dress, together with the ornament filling the spaces between, reduce the harsh and cool two-dimensional
figure of Christ dominating the center of the composition.

PAINTER OF KALENIĆ. *Marriage of Cana.*   *p. 86*
Upon her defeat on the battlefield of Kosovo in 1389, Serbia lost her political
independence and became a vassal state of the Ottoman Empire; but in the
sphere of art it was precisely this sad event that paradoxically for the first time
awakened her to full cultural independence and made her discover her own
genuine style. The best and finest elements of her national traditions were in-
fused with the noble aspirations of the moment, prevalent at the court of the
despot Stephen Lazarević, and reflected on the walls of the churches founded
by his vassals.

The Marriage of Cana is entirely dominated by blue and saffron, and illuminated by the warm atmosphere of pure poetry. Not Christ nor the Virgin Mary, but
the newly married couple occupy the center of the composition. The bride-
groom with tender attention pricks the fingers of his bride with his knife, to
mingle her blood with his own in the ancient pagan fashion. The worldly character of this scene is emphasized both by the elegance of the figures, and by the
rich clothing, their aristocratic gestures and the bright, transparent colors. The
intense yellow, combined with blue and chestnut tones, adds an ethereal note
to this decorative sensuous painting, which is, in fact, far from joyful. There is
a restrained sadness in the bowing heads of the young couple, a weariness in
the gestures of their young hands, and a premature, undefined anxiety in their
faces. The painter seems to be representing a kind of Lord's Supper, whose
participants are all aware of the tragic events that the future holds in store: the
final collapse of their state and the long winter sleep in its creative activity.

SERBIAN SECULAR EMBROIDERY
Cloak of King Milutin
Beginning of 14th century
Silk, embroidered with gold, silver and silk
thread; 28 1/2″ x 56 1/2″
(The inscription between Christ's legs is in Ser-
bian and reads: "God, remember the soul of
your slave Milutin Uroša").
Belgrade, Museum of the Serbian Orthodox
Church

PAINTER OF KALENIĆ
Marriage of Cana
Detail
Circa 1410
Fresco on the south wall of the naos of Intro-
duction Church, Kalenić
(This church was founded by the protovestiary
Bogdan, his wife Milica and his brother Peter).
Kalenić near Rekovac, Serbia, Church of the
Introduction
Belgrade, Fresco Gallery (copy)

PETER SMEDEREVAC. *Crucifixion.* p. 87

This outstanding masterpiece of ancient Serbian embossed silver combines the
style of Italo-Cretan icons with the traditions of the Morava school of painting.
The iconography of this *Crucifixion* is taken from Post-Byzantine miniatures
and icons of the early 16th century, but its elaborate decoration, heightened by
the great number of figures, the unusual gestures and the profusion of ornament in all intermediate spaces, recall the much earlier monuments of Serbian
painting, dating from the first decades of the 15th century. This fusion of ornamental and figurative motifs, of decorative and naturalistic details, brings Peter
Smederevac's *Crucifixion* close to the creations of late Gothic art, underlining
even more clearly the eclecticism of his style.

POST-BYZANTINE PAINTING. *Embrace of the*
                        Apostles Peter and Paul   p. 88

The year 1453, fateful in the history of Constantinople and the Byzantine Empire, was in no way decisive in Byzantine painting. The style of the last Paleologues was persistently cherished in the world of Eastern Christianity, and to
some extent on the island of Crete, and in Venice even up to the beginning of
the 18th century. This icon from the church of Topla combines a favorite subject of late Byzantine art with the circular form of the "tondo", popular in Ital-

PETER SMEDEREVAC
Crucifixion
1540
Gilt silver; 18 3/8" x 11 1/4"
Front cover of the Gospel of St. Maxim the
Bishop.
Belgrade, Museum of the Serbian Orthodox
Church

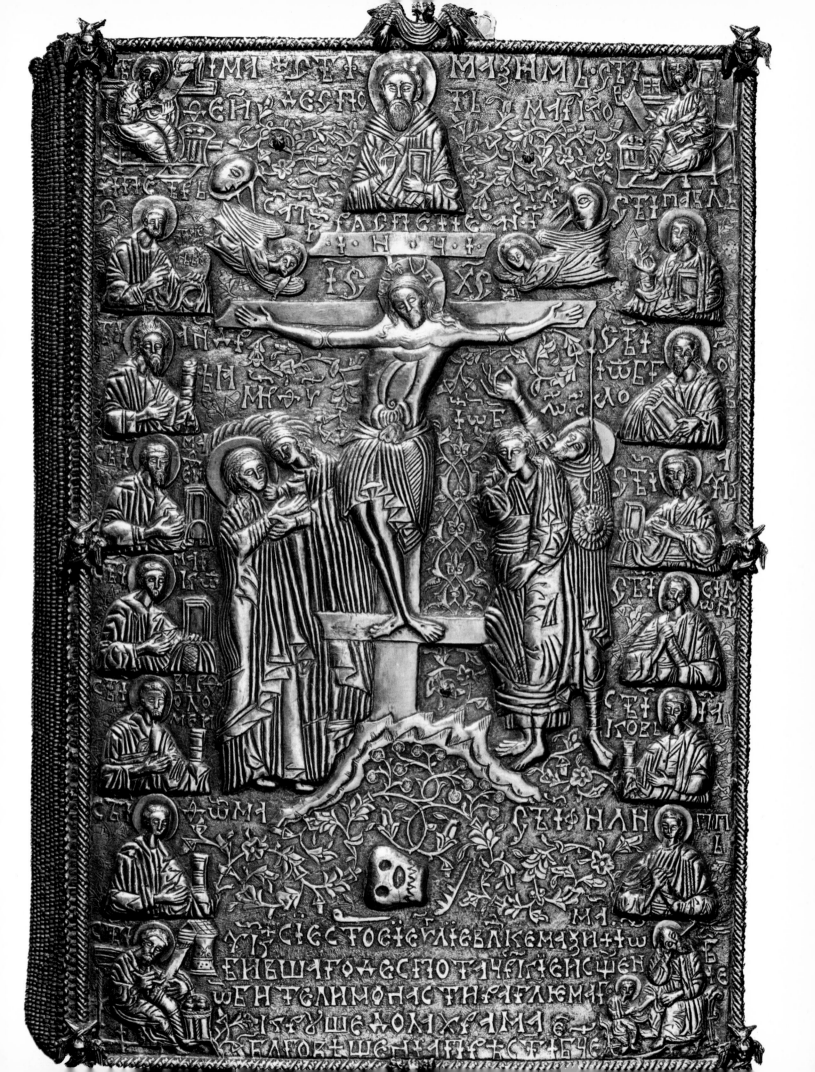

ian Renaissance painting. By its careful elaboration of details and its calligraphic drawing, it belongs stylistically to the circle of Post-Byzantine Cretan painting. The faces of the apostles are individualized and successfully composed within the tondo form, but their embrace is unconvincing and deprived of warmth.

POST–BYZANTINE PAINTING
Embrace of the Apostles Peter and Paul
Second half of 16th century
Tempera on wood; diameter 17 3/4″
Topla near Herceg Novi, Orthodox Church

MOUNT ATHOS ICON PAINTER.   *St. Sava and St. Simeon the Serbian.*   p. 89

This icon representing *St. Sava and St. Simeon* was painted in the monastic environment of Mount Athos, roughly contemporary with the frescoes of Manasija, Serbia's last great medieval church. By its intensity of colors and clarity of draftsmanship, this painting is close to the style of the Morava school; but it is distinguished from the latter by its pronounced realism, its strong contrasts between light and dark, and its simple composition against a neutral background. The saints are frontally represented, and the massive figures with impressionistically modelled heads are not harmonized with the golden-toned background.

MOUNT ATHOS ICON PAINTER
St. Sava and St. Simeon the Serbian
Beginning of 15th century
Tempera painting on wood; 12 3/4″ x 10 1/4″
(This icon probably originates from the Serbian monastery of Hilandar, Mount Athos).
Belgrade, National Museum

BOSNIAN TOMBSTONE ART. *Milutin the Guest.*

Far from the great cultural centers and outside the mainstream of the international medieval styles—Byzantine, Romanesque, Gothic—a specific art form developed in the southwestern regions of the Balkans, chiefly in the territory of Bosnia-Herzegovina, during the 13th to 16th centuries. Its main expression was the relief decoration of the *"stećaks"*—a type of monumental tombstones.

The inscription on the *Stećak of Milutin the Guest* discloses that the deceased was a dignitary of the Bosnian church, was welcomed at the court and heaped with presents from both the native and the Greek nobility. Though he was buried in a sumptuous robe of brocade embroidered with gold, the stone-mason represented Milutin in modest clothing, and of all his numerous possessions he depicts only those that bear a relation to his spiritual wealth: a Gospel book and a staff. The body is haggard, almost fleshless, and the face is inexpressive, more reminiscent of a skull; but the lively, mobile arms end in unnaturally large hands. Hands like these appear on almost all *stećaks,* and are without doubt the most remarkable tribute to human hand paid in all European art. It can be said that since the time of Paleolithic paintings this is the only instance in which the hand with outstretched fingers is considered the measure of human worth. No other details on the *stećaks* are as distinctive. But neither the figural nor the ornamental motifs, carved in low relief on the large blocks of stone which seem to grow so naturally out of the soil and the landscape, stand out; they appear to be their very components—more like rocks eroded by wind and rain over which falls the shadow of a flower, a grape-trellis, a solitary tree, a chance by-passer. The *stećaks* scattered all over Bosnia and Herzegovina have a counterpart only in the prehistoric necropoles of Western Europe and their menhirs; in both, death seems to have been accepted without rational resistance.

BOSNIAN TOMBSTONE ART
Milutin the Guest
15th century
Height 100″
(Cubical monolith with relief decoration and inscription. The front and back of the tombstone represent respectively the deceased, Milutin the Guest, and a large rosette, while the sides show an unclear motif, possibly an interwoven band. This monument is from the hill of Humsko near Foča).
Sarajevo, Regional Museum

BOSNIAN TOMBSTONE ART. *Procession of Knights and Hunting Scenes* p. 91

In Donja Zgošća, not far from the residence of the Bosnian kings, the grave of a courtier interred in the first half of the 15th century is marked by a huge tombstone set on a platform. The profusion and beauty of its relief decorations makes it the outstanding medieval tombstone of Bosnia; but the iconography of these decorations is not typical of *stećak* art. It derives from the artistic achievements of Western Europe, above all the style of late Gothic.

The *Stecak at Donja Zgošćá* is probably not the product of a local stone-cutter. It lacks the basic distinctions of *stećak* art: instead of the isolated symbols, strange human figures with crossed or uplifted arms, and enigmatic compositions, this tombstone depicts armored knights on their horses, tournaments and

BOSNIAN TOMBSTONE ART
Procession of Knights and Hunting Scenes
Middle of 15th century
Stone; 104″ x 54 3/4″ x 66 1/2″
Sculptured top block, placed on a socle, found in Donja Zgošća. (On one side of the tombstone are shown armored knights on horses in the upper frieze, and a hunting scene with a stag and a boar in the lower. The other side is divided into ten fields filled with decorative motifs and figures of mounted knights. The front shows a castle, its owners, their servants and saddled horses. The back is covered with ornaments.)
Sarajevo, Regional Museum

hunting scenes on a succession of friezes and metopes recalling tapestries in the castles of Western Europe. All the figures are shown in action and are logically interrelated. The usual mystic atmosphere of *stećaks* is replaced by worldliness, and the symbolic language of oracular statement by outright narration. Even the ornament is not freely placed, but organized into zones and fields, and thereby reduced to simple decoration. It is an open question whether the hunting scenes have a deeper, symbolic meaning. On a Merovingian sarcophagus, for instance, a deer would represent the deceased, and the hunter would signify death. Here, the action taking place around the three trees in the lower frieze might illustrate the fight with the dark powers of life, and the liberation from this fight brought by death. But this is a commonplace in European medieval art.

91

ISLAMIC MINIATURES.   *Signs of the Zodiac.*

These two miniatures representing the *Signs of the Zodiac*—Sun in the sign of Aries, in opposition with Saturn and Mars; Sun in the sign of Sagittarius, in opposition with Jupiter and the Moon—are composite in detail and eclectic in style, reflecting the exuberant oriental world under Mongolian rule. Beneath the sign of the zodiac, shown in the upper part of the composition, the planets are pictured in small rectangular fields: in the left-hand miniature, Mars is a youthful Mongolian warrior, Saturn a half-naked old man with an ax on his shoulder, Venus a harem beauty, Jupiter a self-contented courier, Mercury an imperial clerk. All the figures are represented in the tradition of two-dimensional painting of the Mesopotamian school, without any indication of volume or spatial depth. More care has been lavished on the clothes and arms than on the physiognomies, which are invariably stereotyped and inexpressive, or on the gestures, which are monotonously repeated again and again. Most of the ele-

ISLAMIC MINIATURES
Signs of the Zodiac
First half of 15th century
Gold and tempera on paper; 10 1/4″ x 6 5/8″
(Two of ten miniatures from a fragmentary Islamic treatise on astrology, from Turkey).
Sarajevo, Oriental Institute

PERSIAN MINIATURE
Lukhrasp Fighting the Turks
1573
Gold and tempera painting on paper; 15″ x 9 7/8″
(One of the twenty miniatures illustrating Firdusi's *Book of Kings,* from the collection of Baron Franz Ottenfels Taliq script).
Zagreb, State Archives

ments are Mongolian, though some details are taken from the Buddhist art of India. The color is rich, but shadows are indicated by hatches, so that the various hues appear uncompromisingly flat, and all the surfaces are clearly determined just as the human destinies described in the book.

PERSIAN MINIATURE. *Lukhrasp Fighting the Turks.*   *p. 93*
This scene of *Lukhrasp Fighting the Turks* is pictured in the best traditions of
the refined style of Persian miniature painting, cultivated in Shiraz and Herat at
the end of the 14th and the beginning of the 15th centuries. The brilliant colors
and the system of vertical perspective, crowned by the wavy contour of the hill
in the background, are characteristic of the Shiraz school, but the small figures
on gracile horses, the elaboration of details and the pronounced emphasis on
decoration link this miniature to the lighter, more transparent style of the Sa-
favid dynasty, already prefigured by the miniatures painted in Herat and Tabris
by the famous master Bikhzad. The congested grouping of the horsemen, cut
off by the edges of the miniature, flank the large battlefield and draw attention
to the protagonists in the dynamic fight at the center of the composition, a
treatment strongly reminiscent of Paolo Uccello's battle and hunting scenes:
they show the same obsession with geometry, the same "disciplined turmoil."

THE SARAJEVO HAGADA. *Rabbi Gamaliel with His Disciples*   *p. 95*
With its sure drawing and lively, contrasting colors (chiefly blue and vermil-
ion), *Rabbi Gamaliel with His Disciples,* is one of the most beautiful and typical
of medieval Jewish miniatures. The subject is apparently inspired by illuminations from the ancient codices of the Hebrew Bible, and is consistent with the
character of the corresponding text, which is read in Jewish homes on the eve
of Passover, a ritual in which both adults and children participated. The didac-
tic tone, the seriousness and the simplicity of the scene indicate that the artist
himself was a Jew; but everything else—the technique, the selection and composition of the colors, the drawing, the arrangement of the figures and their relation towards the background—is borrowed from the medieval art of Western
Europe, although it was only in Germany, France or Spain that a member of a
Jewish community could have seen such examples. By the disposition of its illuminations, the *Sarajevo Hagada* belongs to the Spanish-Provençal group of
Jewish ritual books. The style of the miniatures is eclectic: Rabbi Gamaliel with
his three disciples is set in front of a stereotyped background, like in Italian
Trecento art; but the restricted color scale and the absence of perspective
clearly indicate that the dominant influence is French Gothic.

THE SARAJEVO HAGADA
Rabbi Gamaliel with His Disciples
About 1360
Tempera on parchment; 6 1/4" x 8 5/8"
(Miniature on page 25 of the *Sarajevo Hagada,*
Hebrew book of ritual).
Sarajevo, Regional Museum

SCHOOL OF AVIGNON. *St. Peter Enthroned.*   *p. 96*
Thanks to the "Babylonish Exile" of the popes, one of the most astonishing
schools of art sprang up in Avignon between 1309 and 1424; its language of expression was at first molded by the Italian Trecento (Simone Martini, Lippo
Memmi), then by northern Gothic, to become at last, in the course of the 15th
century, original and international, by fusing the best traditions of Italy, France
and Flanders. It is difficult to determine to which of the numerous Avignon artists the painting of *St. Peter Enthroned* at the Strossmayer gallery can be as-
cribed. The author of this work is distinguished by a sense of materiality peculiar to Flemish painting. He knows how to emphasize the volume of the figure;
but while the saint's head is modelled with a realistic depth that predicts the
portrait painting of Nicolas Froment and Jean Fouquet, the folds of his clothing
are rendered in an archaic, typically Gothic manner.

SCHOOL OF AVIGNON
St. Peter Enthroned
Beginning of 15th century
Tempera on wood; 69 1/4″ x 34 1/2″
Zagreb, Strossmayer Gallery (Collection of
Ante Topić Mimara)

PAOLO VENEZIANO. *Polyptych of St. Lucy.*

Just as the beauty of Venice is a mixture of influences and treasures from distant regions of Europe and Asia, so the personal style of Paolo Veneziano, the founder of Venetian painting, was formed from disparate, foreign elements. At the moment when Paolo was starting out, the church of Murano was decorated in the purest spirit of Paleologue art, while the local workshops either cultivated the ancient Byzantine style, or fancied a Romanesque that was gradually swerving towards Gothic. It was far from easy to fuse these divergent currents into one. On the *Polyptych of St. Lucy* they are still stratified rather than harmonized; but they already combine into a new, complete organism. The outside shell is Gothic, the expression Romanesque, the setting Byzantine, but the clear contours drawn in red and grey and the lively colors are peculiar only to Paolo Veneziano.

In the central panel stands the monumental, hieratic figure of St. Lucy. The

PAOLO VENEZIANO
(?–1362)
Polyptych of St. Lucy
Ca. 1330
Gold and tempera on wood; 57 1/2″ x 67″
Krk, Episcopal Ordinatoriate

97

PRECURSOR OF PAOLO VENEZIANO
Altar Pall of the Blessed Leon Bembo
1321
Gold and tempera on wood; 30″ x 65 3/8″
Vodnjan, Istria, Parish Church of St. Blasius

eight panels to the left and the right offer a lively account of the main events of the saint's life. The prominent top section shows the scene of the Annunciation intersected by that of the Crucifixion, while the slightly lower trilobes represent St. Quirinus, St. John, St. Andrew and St. Gaudentius. The gold background, the linear folds of the draperies and the large surfaces give an archaic effect; but the lively details show Paolo's sense of reality.

PAOLO VENEZIANO. *Birth of Christ.*   *p. 98*
The *Birth of Christ* is one of the loftiest, most lyrical creations of Venetian painting of the 14th century. The free realistic narration, the clear drawing and the skillful composition in this work are permeated by a refined sensibility—so remarkable that the experts are still hesitant whether to ascribe its authorship to Paolo or to Lorenzo Veneziano. In the center of the picture, out of a cave in the bare rock, a new being radiates, warmed by maternal tenderness and the breath of animals, while the earth glows in exultation at the fulfillment of the great promise. As if rain had fallen on the parched soil, a rejuvenated life, endowed with solid forms and intense colors, spouts from all the crevices of the rock. In the foreground, St. Joseph and a shepherd are shown in lively conversation near a flock of sheep, while on the barren slopes two other shepherds and a group of angels, in vestments of blue, red, green, violet and yellow, form two rhythmically opposed currents—rising on the left, rising-and-falling on the right. This positive gradation is also accentuated by the individualized physiognomies and even by the varied folds of the clothing. St. Joseph and the shepherds are presented realistically, while the Virgin is idealized by the folds of her dress highlighted in dense gold lines; the gracile figures of the angels, painted with consummate delicacy, crown the composition in a mood of glory and

PAOLO VENEZIANO
Birth of Christ
Ca. 1355
Gold and tempera on wood; 26 3/4″ x 21 5/8″
Belgrade, National Museum

FRANCESCO DA MILANO
(Sesto near Milan?—Zadar?)
Tempest at Sea
Detail from the Reliquary of St. Simon
1380
Gilt-silver plate; dimensions of the reliquary;
76 3/8″ x 50″ x 31 1/2″
(The reliquary is a gift of queen Elizabeth Ko-
tromanić, wife of Ludwig the Great, to the
Church of St. Simon, Zadar).
Zadar, Church of St. Simon

undisturbed serenity. But the basic value of the picture is in its central concept, in the presentation of the birth of the miraculous child out of the desolate rock wall. The painter joyfully communicates the idea of a new, vigorous life springing up where the human mind would least expect it.

PRECURSOR OF PAOLO VENEZIANO.   *Altar Pall of the*
Blessed Leone Bembo.   *p. 99*

This *Altar Pall* from Vodnjan indicates that an exceptionally gifted painter was at work in Venice in 1321; he undoubtedly was familiar with Sienese and Florentine painting, above all Giotto's achievements in Padua, Ferrara, Ravenna and Rimini. Within the framework of five fields, in a style of realistic expressiveness and warm color, and by means of sculpturesque figures moving freely against a background of Romanesque architecture painted in perspective—he depicts the legend of the venerated Venetian saint Leone Bembo: the astonished believers discovering the saint's unchanged body in the sarcophagus; bishops, monks and citizens repentantly praying over it; the saint returning the eyesight of a blind girl; and restoring a paralyzed girl. The monumental, tranquil figure of the miracle worker in the central field balances the varied rhythms and appeases the heterogeneous emotions expressed in the flanking panels.

FOLLOWER OF JOHANNES AQUILA
The Apostles
1383
Frescoes in the parish house of the old church
at Turnišće, Prekmurje.
Ljubljana, National Gallery (copy)

FRANCESCO DA MILANO. *Tempest at Sea.* *p. 100*

European art of the second half of the 14th century is characterized by more or less successful compilations of traditional stylistic solutions. This long stagnation is less apparent in miniatures, tapestries and paintings than in the creations of monumental art. This is quite understandable, for to fulfill the most varied, sometimes quite specific demands of a customer ordering a reliquary or a decorative textile, the artist could not always find suitable sources in tradition. To illustrate the legend connected with the relics of St. Simon, and at the request of the donor connected with certain well-known historical personalities, Francesco da Milano made use of Giotto's original composition, and applied the Gothic procedure of rendering a religious subject in terms of a concrete situation of real life. *Tempest at Sea* represents an event which—like in Giotto's paintings—is clearly determined in time and space: St. Simon himself saves the ship carrying his relics from Venice to Zadar, from the malignant spirit of the tempest. The figures are arranged exactly along the diagonals of the square field formed by the silver plate, but the high waves of the turbulent sea make a lively curve in the lower part of the composition, which is repeated and even

intensified by the dynamic gesturing of the sailors. The massiveness of the waves and of the strained sail is emphasized in the spirit of northern Gothic, which is also evoked by the active, implicit relation between man and extraterrestrial forces. The deliverance of the boat is not only the result of St. Simon's outstretched hand, but also due to the endeavors of the sailors; so that man here becomes one of the partakers of the miracle.

FOLLOWER OF JOHANNES AQUILA. *The Apostles.* *p. 101*
The Apostles from Turnišće are a late echo of the highly developed realistic style, formed in Bohemia at the court of Charles IV from a fusion of the traditions of Giotto's painting and High Gothic. Owing to the activity of Tommaso da Modena, master Theodorich and Peter Parler, Prague became the leading art

LATE GOTHIC CARVING
Predella of St. Andrew
Circa 1500
Fir and poplar woodcarving; 50″ x 29 3/8″ x 9 1/2″
Originating from Gosteče near Škofja Loka.
Ljubljana, National Gallery

center of Europe, from where the new style of Late Gothic spread toward the west. Through Vienna and the Tyrol it reached the Prekmurje region, where the painter and architect Johannes Aquila of Radgona was active in the last quarter of the 14th century. An unidentified follower who in 1483 decorated the parish house of the old church of Turnišče, was clearly inspired by Bohemian painting. His figures are individualized and imbued with material, firm volumes. The row of apostles is stably set in space. Thanks to the skillfully composed movements, a natural link has been established between them, and in spite of the unchanging pattern of the eyes, each figure is given some characteristic of its own. By the arrangement of color, the continuous rhythm of the folds of the drapery, gestures of the hands and positions of the heads, a lively dialogue between the figures is suggested; this must have been an attraction to the common people, whose influence was already strongly felt in the society of the late Middle Ages.

LATE GOTHIC CARVING. *Predella of St. Andrew.* p. 102

Simplicity of composition and an archaic style distinguish the high relief decoration of this *Predella* from Gosteče. It is attributed to Jakob of Loka, a woodcarver in whose productions the mannerism of late Gothic is still enlivened by realistic traditions. The realism achieved in the modelling of the saints' heads, especially those of St. Peter and the holy hermit, is contrasted with the conscientious stylization of the folds of the clothes. The naïvely represented feet, the stressed parallel lines of the drapery and the harsh, simplified contours deprive the figures of volume, and any fluency or lyricism is totally lacking. This archaistic current in late Gothic art is actually a reaction to the intrusion of the Renaissance into the Alpine regions, a last resistance before the definite acceptance of a new, classicist style.

CARINTHIAN WOODCARVER
Virgin and Child
Circa 1510
Polychrome limewood carving; height 30 3/4"
Originating from Radlje ob Dravi, Slovenia.
Ljubljana, National Gallery

CARINTHIAN WOODCARVING. *Virgin and Child.*

Although a 16th-century work, this *Virgin and Child* clearly recalls the "beautiful Madonnas" of a century earlier. Her sweet, childlike head and her ample mantle with its soft folds arranged without clear relation to the position of the body show that in Carinthia prior to the complete adoption of the classic Renaissance concept of form, the late Gothic realistic tradition was in retreat in favor of the gentler, more delicate style of the Viennese school. Except for the calligraphically stylized folds, the basic lines flow quietly and almost parallel, while the slight inclination of the Virgin's head and her sensitively carved hands are the only restless features of this melodiously modelled sculpture.

VINCENT OF KASTAV. *Prayer in the Garden of Gethsemane.* p. 104
The *Prayer in the Garden of Gethsemane*—the complete solitude of a human soul in mortal anguish—is represented in the modest church of St. Mary near Beram as an impressive, painful dream, in which everything that is separate in time and place in the real world is brought together as a single experience, in which every sound seems to resound clearly and every detail appears illuminated by intense light: the smallest leaf of grass and the tiniest blossom, the pegs of the wooden fence and the drops of sweat on the body of Christ exhausted by prayer. In the immediate vicinity, in Venice, Giovanni Bellini painted the same subject about 1470, but his rationalist catharsis would be incomprehensible to the Istrian painter, who with the frank candor of a man of the people literally accepts the touching account of the Evangelist, and searches for adequate stylistic solutions not in the south, but in the north, in the regional painting of the Subalpine region, above all of the Tyrol, where remnants of the "soft style" and idealism of Gothic art still survived, blending with the new, veristic accents struck by German and Dutch art. But under the Istrian sky this continental style was dematerialized and condensed. The sculpturesque Gothic folds are transformed into angular ornamental furrows, the colors are spread out over the large, two-dimensional surfaces, while the mountains and figures in the background are brought forward to the first plane, as on a bright, transparent morning. On the other hand, the figures, actions and details are so numerous that they pierce the frame of the picture. The painter wishes to convey everything at the same time: Christ's feverish prayer, the sleeping disciples, the stealthy steps of Judas. With the directness of a Mediterranean, he accepts even the metaphor of St. Luke's Gospel as literal truth: he paints the drops of sweat on Christ's body as drops of blood, and indicates the deep sleep of St. Peter, St. James and St. John by their large, heavy eyelids.

IVAN OF KASTAV
Adam and Eve at Work
1490
Fresco on the vault of the central nave of the
Trinity Chapel, Hrastovlje.
Hrastovlje, Istria, Trinity Chapel

VINCENT OF KASTAV
Prayer in the Garden of Gethsemane
1474
Fresco on the north wall of the Church of St.
Mary "Na Škrilinah".
Beram, Istria, St. Mary's Church

IVAN OF KASTAV. *Adam and Eve at Work.*
The decoration of Trinity Chapel at Hrastovlje—the last great medieval fresco ensemble of Istria—was executed by Ivan of Kastav and his assistants in the spirit of the local tradition combined with that of the more progressive painting of the Tyrolean master Jakob Sunter. By its drawing and color *Adam and Eve at Work* is linked with the earlier frescoes of Istria, above all those of St. Mary's church near Beram; but its general atmosphere, which is deprived of any Gothic idealism or aristocratic refinement, is close to the rustic realism of Sunter's Tyrolean school of painting. Adam tilling the earth in his sweat, and Eve giving her breasts to a pair of twins and spinning at the same time, together with the cooking-vessels, the swaddling clothes and the modest cottage, are quite as important to the painter as the figure of God represented as an indifferent observer in the background. This objective narration, without any climaxes or drama, the ugly children in Eve's lap and the broken folds of her dress show that Ivan of Kastav was also acquainted with Dutch prints.

MASTER OF THE EGGENBERG ALTAR
St. Ann
Circa 1485
Painted limewood carving; height 49 5/8"
Originating from Radgona
Ljubljana, National Gallery

p. 107
PAINTER OF ST. PRIMUS CHURCH
The Virgin Mary at the Loom
1504
Tempera on wood
One of the twelve scenes illustrating the life of
the Virgin on the southern wall of the Church of
St. Primus.
St. Primus Church near Kamnik, Slovenia
Ljubljana, National Gallery (copy)

MASTER OF THE EGGENBERG ALTAR. *St. Ann.*

Almost all the sculptures produced in the Alpine regions of the Tyrol and the surrounding provinces in the last quarter of the 14th century are stylistically linked to the creations of the workshop of Michael Pacher, an artist who combined the rationalism of the early Renaissance with the emotivity of Central European Gothic. The creator of this monumental figure of *St. Ann,* supposed to be also the author of the statues of the Virgin from Waldstein and Eggenberg, was evidently familiar with Pacher's carved altars. But instead of their perspective solutions of depth and lyrical modulation, he develops his composition in relief and introduces in the face of St. Ann the traits of provincial portrait realism, probably inspired by the work of the Dutch printmaker known as the Master ''E.S.'' The basic mass is firmly established by a solid contour, but within this frame the folds of the dress and the moving figures in the lap of St. Ann create strong contrasts of light and shade, and give the entire group an almost baroque dynamism and picturesqueness.

PAINTER OF ST. PRIMUS CHURCH. *The Virgin Mary at the Loom.* p. 107

The frescoes on the north and south walls of St. Primus Church near Kamnik (Sv. Primož pri Kamniku) mark the decisive moment when the structure of Gothic art was undermined and the spirit of Renaissance art accepted on Slovenian territory. The twenty scenes from the life of the Virgin are painted under the influence of medieval apocryphal literature and according to the traditional iconographic schemes, but with a new serenity, in a new space and new lighting, without the restlessness of late Gothic. Though the perspective is not founded on the scientific optical theories of Italian Renaissance, the interior in which the Virgin is shown weaving a curtain for a temple, possesses both definition and spatial depth; and the light, though not emanating from any determined point, appears far from unreal, for it glides mildly over the surfaces of the forms and illuminates them with a soft glow. The woman assiduously embroidering in the right foreground, and the girl behind her unravelling the thread and watching the work with great interest, are represented with a charming blend of realism and pure poetry.

PAINTER OF ST. PRIMUS CHURCH. *Procession of the Magi.* p. 108

The huge composition representing the *Procession of the Magi* in the form of one uninterrupted picture, narrates with great detail the events from the parting of the Magi from Herod in Jerusalem to their tribute to Christ in Bethlehem. The continuity of this scene is archaic and the iconography traditional, but the rhythm which pervades it is new, as is the realism of the individual scenes and characters. Along the narrow band connecting Jerusalem with Bethlehem, the figures are skillfully arranged: the dynamics of the masses grow and culminate in the center of the composition, where the second of the Magi is shown on horseback, with his precious gifts and his suite, while towards the end of the picture everything calms down into the devout reverence of the third of the Magi at the feet of Christ. The large surfaces covered with red, yellow, green,

PAINTER OF ST. PRIMUS CHURCH
Procession of the Magi (detail)
1504
Fresco on the north wall of the Church of St. Primus
Length of fresco: 38′
St. Primus Church near Kamnik, Slovenia

violet and white give the painting a fresh, summery tone, while some exceptional genre scenes—for instance the servants gazing enraptured at the star surmounting Bethlehem, the fat cook with a basket filled to the brim with eggs, or the court fool offering drink to the piper—are represented with convincing realism and a sincere interest in man, in the best spirit of the German Renaissance.

PART IV
LATER CENTURIES
(Idealism to Naturalism)

BARTOLOMEO CAPORALI
Perugia, circa 1420–circa 1505
Virgin with Christ, Saints and Angels (1464)
Tempera and gold on lime-wood; 17 1/8″ × 12 1/2″
Zagreb, Strossmayer Gallery

BARTOLOMEO CAPORALI.   *Virgin with Christ, Saints and Angels.*

The deep piety and the traditions of the pre-Renaissance art of Umbria, home of St. Francis of Assisi and Gentile da Fabriano, are still alive in the style of Bartolomeo Caporali. Although in the high tide of Quattrocento painting— while the Florentine artists, in the footsteps of Donatello and Masaccio, were developing plastic form in three-dimensional space—Caporali continues to represent rigidly modelled figures of the Virgin, saints and angels on a gold background enlivened by incised designs. The Christ child and the angels are depicted with rosy, fresh, beautiful Umbrian faces framed by fair hair. The Virgin is first of all a saint and only incidentally a mother, while the emaciated figures of St. Francis and St. Benedict are set in the foreground like two strong, austere pillars sustaining the teaching of Christ. The pronounced symmetry of the composition has been handed down from Perugino, the rational austerity of forms from Piero della Francesca, the vivid colors from Benozzo Gozzoli.

FRA ANGELICO
(GIOVANNI DA FIESOLE)
Vicchio di Mugello 1387–Rome 1455
Stigmatization of St. Francis and
Death of St. Peter the Martyr
Tempera and gold on lime-wood; 9 1/2″ x 17 1/4″
Zagreb, Strossmayer Gallery

FRA ANGELICO. *Stigmatization of St. Francis and*
Death of St. Peter the Martyr.

In the revival of Florentine art of the 15th century, Beato Angelico holds a special place. He felt closer to medieval miniatures, to Masolino's paintings pervaded by the spirit of the International Gothic and devout composure, than to the bold style of a Masaccio or a Donatello, their dramatic revolt and their persistent search into the complexities of reality. As a Dominican sincerely devoted to the principal task of his order, namely to preach the word of God, Beato Angelico throughout his life painted nothing but beautiful sermons. Even in depicting painful and dramatic subjects, the artist could cover them with a profusion of flowers and bathe them in a tender light. On the small panel in the Strossmayer Gallery, shrubs shoot up and flower out of the blood of St. Peter the Martyr in the foreground, while beyond the ecstasy of St. Francis a radiant light shines on the tree-tops and hills of the background. In the foreground the

111

LOVRO DOBRIČEVIĆ
(LOVRO MARINOV)
Kotor 1420–Dubrovnik 1478
Polyptych (1448)
Tempera and gold on wood; 98″ x 101″
(Late Gothic oak frame by the Dubrovnik
woodcarver and painter Marko Junčić).
Dubrovnik, Dominican Monastery

executioner's knife fails to quell the religious fervor of the martyr, who continues to inscribe the words CREDO IN UNUM D . . . in the sand, while the
approach of an armed band does not interrupt the ardent prayer of the Dominican standing at the entrance of the cave; and in an extension of the same landscape a fairy-tale crown of red and gold hovers above the roof of a little chapel,
while·in the very same colors, in the guise of a miraculous bird, Christ appears
in dazzling splendor showering his stigmas on St. Francis. The graphic draftsmanship, the composition all in one plane and the immediacy of this painting,
small in size but large in effect, seem to confirm Vasari's supposition that Beato
Angelico was originally apprenticed as a miniaturist.

LOVRO DOBRIČEVIĆ. *Polyptych.* *p. 112*

On the coasts of the Adriatic, the dawn of Renaissance art was slow to appear. In Dubrovnik, just like in Venice and Murano, the winding Gothic outlines on the traditional gold backgrounds began to straighten up only in the second quarter of the 15th century. Twenty more years had to pass before the figures began to move in a spatially determined landscape.

Lovro Dobričević was born on the coast, in Kotor. He acquired his knowledge of painting in the lagoon city and eagerly collected ancient sculptures; but in this, his first important work, the *Polyptych* painted for the Dominican Church in Dubrovnik, there is no trace of the luminous Dalmatian sky or of moving, plastic forms. The intricate oak frames of his panels were carved by Matko Junčić, who followed in the footsteps of Lorenzo Veneziano; the iconography of the *Polyptych,* too, is linked with the traditions of 14th-century Venetian art—in particular the saints flanking Christ's Baptism in the lower zone and the Virgin with Christ in the upper zone. The figures are conventional in the spirit of Gothic art: the younger saints are idealized. But a tenderness quite unknown to the Gothic emanates from the center of the *Polyptych.* In the scene of Baptism, we can discern a green river flowing among blue banks and bathing the feet of the naked figure of Christ.

LOVRO DOBRIČEVIĆ. *St. Julian.*

Only the works from his riper age prove that Lovro Dobričević was endowed with a mind of the humanist pattern and a developed sense of reality; this applies, above all, to the figure of *St. Julian* in his *Polyptych* executed for St. Mary's Church, Danče. The noble figure, with intelligent eyes and sensual lips, could be met in the streets of Dubrovnik, among the duke's courtiers, or in a church during the celebration of a solemn mass. The saint's head is certainly a portrait, softly modelled with sensitive lines and half-tones, which express an almost boyish virtue together with fear in facing the realities of life. The other figures of this *Polyptych* (Virgin in Glory, with Christ in her lap, dominated by the bust of God the Father, surrounded by angel choirs and flanked by saints), painted under the influence of the Vivarini brothers, are similarly free of rigid linearism; but *St. Julian* stands out as the most convincingly lifelike.

COSIMO ROSSELLI. *Virgin and Child with Two Angels.* *p. 114*

Rosselli's *Virgin and Child with Two Angels,* with its simple composition and harmonious colors, possesses a distinction that can explain why its author, otherwise considered a minor Florentine painter, was called to Rome in 1481 to decorate the walls of the Sistine Chapel, together with Botticelli, Ghirlandaio and Perugino. The eclecticism of Rosselli's style is unobtrusive here; the artist has liberated himself from the crude late-Gothic archaism of his master Neri di Bicci; he has softened the glaring light-effects of Domenico Veneziano and to a considerable extent reduced the painful turmoil of Botticelli and Filippino Lippi. This beautiful picture is suffused with the sadness of imminent parting. The infant Christ is forcibly wresting himself out of the Virgin's embrace, barely touching her with his hands, turning his head away and casting his enraptured look upwards, as if accepting great tasks from his heavenly father. The bowing angels join in the mother's pain; her light embrace is full of self-renouncement. All this is expressed with utter restraint, without pathos, in a dignified tone which approaches the art of High Renaissance.

LOVRO DOBRIČEVIĆ
(LOVRO MARINOV)
St. Julian (1465)
Tempera and gold on wood
Detail of a polyptych.
Dubrovnik, Church of Danče

COSIMO ROSSELLI
Florence 1439–1507
Virgin and Child with Two Angels
Tempera on wood; 27 1/4" x 18 1/4"
Zagreb, Strossmayer Gallery

PIER FRANCESCO FIORENTINO. *God the Father and the Virgin with Christ and St. John.* p. 115

Pier Francesco Fiorentino tends to be considered an average painter of the Florentine school of the late Quattrocento, whose workshop mass-produced cursory paintings of the Virgin, using chiefly borrowings from the works of Fra Filippo Lippi and Francesco Pesellino. But it has not yet been sufficiently recognized that Fiorentino, while gathering the cream of other painters' achievements, often knew how to fuse them in a thoroughly new way, to add his own outlines and colors and suffuse them with a light hitherto unknown. This is clearly shown in his picture *God the Father and the Virgin with Christ and St. John.* The figure of God the Father is taken directly from Filippo Lippi (*Homage to Christ* in the Berlin State Museum), but by extending his cloak to embrace the Virgin's shoulders an intimate connection is established between all the figures of the composition, and a strong support erected in the background, which can at the same time explain the painful drama taking place in the foreground. The protagonists of this drama are the Virgin and the Christ child. The boy, with his head drawn in between his shoulders, is firmly holding a bird in his hand, but is uninterested in it, for he is looking out at the world with indescribable anguish. The white of his drapery with its stylized folds suggest a

114

PIER FRANCESCO FIORENTINO
Florence 1444/5–circa 1500
God the Father and the Virgin with Christ and St. John
Tempera on lime-wood; 29 1/4" x 15 3/8"
Zagreb, Strossmayer Gallery

coldness from which his small body revolts, while the Virgin's hands are laid without maternal warmth around the terrified child. The Virgin is resigned; she can already see her son on Mount Calvary, and her pain and helplessness are movingly reflected in the stylized folds of her kerchief, which look like the drooping wings of a wounded bird.

GIOVANNI BELLINI. *St. Nicholas.*

His long life and his lively, receptive mind gave Giovanni Bellini the opportunity of combining the severe, ascetic forms of Jacopo Bellini and Mantegna with the sensuous, colorist painting of Giorgione and Titian. *St. Nicholas* dates from the mature years of the artist's life, slightly earlier than the *Triptych* of 1488 in the church of Santa Maria dei Frari, Venice, when Bellini finally arrived at a balance between the divine and the human in man and nature. The saint is represented as a vigorous old man of flesh and blood, his face deeply furrowed by external and internal struggles. His present tranquillity and devotion to God are an outcome of the restlessness of youth, of the slow ripening and gathering of all kinds of intellectual and sensual experiences. The closed book and the hand mildly resting on his bishop's staff indicate that he has spoken his greatest words and all his chief tasks have been carried out. The saint's head is slightly bowed under the weight of his richly decorated mitre, while the greenish-blue sky troubled by grey clouds creates a deep space in the background, which serves to underline mans's isolation in an indifferent nature. It is characteristic, however, that the material world is strongly emphasized in this picture, together with the psychological drama enacted under patches of Venetian sky.

GIOVANNI BELLINI
Venice, ca. 1430–1516
St. Nicholas (circa 1487)
Tempera and oil on wood; 42 3/4″ x 16 5/8″
Zagreb, Strossmayer Gallery

WORKSHOP OF FILIPPO LIPPI. *The Holy Family with St. John and St. Margaret.* p. 117

It is within a circle—that most perfect and most intimate of all geometric forms—that the *Holy Family with St. John and St. Margaret* is represented in this work. Between two horizontals (the balustrade in the foreground and the horizon in the background) and against one stressed vertical element (architectural element at left center), the composition is confined to triangles of unequal height. The first triangle is formed by the embracing figures of Christ and St. John, the second by the gracefully inclined bodies of the Virgin and St. Margaret, and the third—independent of the others and slightly oblique—by the form of the aged, but still vigorous St. Joseph. This geometrical scheme dominates the refined figures, so characteristic of the paintings of Filippo Lippi. The unknown artist has faithfully reproduced the subtle drawing of that devoted pupil of Botticelli, accepted his warm, transparent colors and tremulous, effective rhythms. The tondo is flooded by elegant forms and movements that render an almost unreal effect. It is a beautiful formula, but with an artificial structure.

WORKSHOP OF FILIPPO LIPPI
The Holy Family with St. John and St. Margaret (circa 1496)
Tempera on lime-wood; diameter 31 7/8″
Zagreb, Strossmayer Gallery

VITTORE CARPACCIO
Venice or Koper, about 1455–Venice 1526
St. Roch (circa 1520)
Tempera and oil on wood; 41 3/4" x 14 1/8"
Belgrade, National Museum

MATTEO DA MILANO
Active in Ferrara between 1502 and 1512
Scenes from the Life of St. Paul (circa 1502–1505)
Watercolor on paper; 13 1/8" x 9 1/8"
(Miniature from the *Breviary* of Duke Ercoles I d'Este of Ferrara).
Zagreb, Strossmayer Gallery

VITTORE CARPACCIO.   *St. Roch.*

Vittore Carpaccio, pupil of Gentile Bellini, impassioned observer of the luxury and misery of Venice, poet of its lagoons, bridges, roofs and piazzettas, creator of great cyclical compositions and the first genre painter of Italian art, in the last years of his life averted his eyes from the maddening spectacle of the world and turned them inward, toward quiet landscapes, mild luminosity and God. Various internal and external factors might have played a decisive part in this change in Carpaccio's style: the intensified religiosity of the aging arts, fatigue and exhausted invention, perhaps also the change of taste of the first decades of the 16th century, and the successes of Giorgione and Titian. *St. Roch* is painted delicately, with soft outlines and in warm colors with gentle transitions. With accent on shadows, in a golden atmosphere that recalls Giorgione, the figure of the young saint loses all definition, and in the skillful movement of head, body and legs Carpaccio seems to have found that "winding, creative axis of form" extolled by Leonardo da Vinci in his *Treatise on Painting.* Though far from being emphasized, this winding axis determines all the shadows and details: the curious, unnatural position of the right eye, the lock of hair on the forehead, the seam of the jacket down the breast, and even the folds of the boots. This is the curve that Bergson considers the key to every figure.

MATTEO DA MILANO.   *Scenes from the Life of St. Paul.*   *p. 119*

Scenes from the Life of St. Paul is one of four miniatures from the breviary of Ercole I d'Este, Duke of Ferrara. The miniatures were bought in Amalfi in 1870, while the text of the *Breviary,* without the illuminations, has been kept in Vienna since 1859. The opinions of art historians on the question of authorship of these miniatures are highly divergent: Adolfo Venturi considers them a work of Gianfrancesco de Maineri; Campori thinks they were painted by Matteo da Milano, Tommaso da Modena and Cesare delle Vieze; Milanesi and Pini ascribe them to Madro; and Hermann attributes them to Matteo da Milano. It is well established, however, that the miniatures were produced in Ferrara before the death of Ercole I, for after 1505 the emblems of duke Alfonso I were added.

Borders of unequal width, profusely decorated with acanthus leaves, unicorns, a fanciful candelabrum, human hippogriffs, bird and medallion motifs, frame a rectangular field, on which, in front of a fabulous Renaissance palace with a cupola, St. Paul is shown awakening his three companions, while the Savior appears in the sky. In spite of the numerous and varied details—the luxurious architectural decoration, the boy in the gallery holding a coat-of-arms of the Este family, the three townsmen under the porch, the deep landscape with passersby, a river, castles, trees and distant hills—the scene can easily be grasped. The fresh, vivid colors, the spirited modelling and the precise drawing place the author of this illumination among the outstanding miniaturists of the Renaissance

NIKOLA BOŽIDAREVIĆ
Krucica, about 1460–Dubrovnik 1517
Triptych (1517)
Tempera on wood; Central part: 72″ x 55 1/2″;
Lunette: 31 1/2″ x 74 3/4″
Dubrovnik, Church of Danče

NIKOLA BOŽIDAREVIĆ. *Triptych.* p. 120, 121

The work of Nikola Božidarević marks the peak of the Dubrovnik school of painting, and its ripest fruit in a hundred years of maturing. Božidarević fused the best he could find in tradition with the new knowledge acquired during his travel to Italy, chiefly in Venice and The Marches region, and instilled it all with the moods reigning in the proud, independent city of Dubrovnik.

The *Triptych* from the church of Danče is a veritable summary of Božidarević's achievements, and to a large extent of the entire Dubrovnik school of painting. The style of International Gothic and of Venetian art of the first half of the 15th century, which was the decisive factor in the rise of Dubrovnik painting, is still mildly reflected in the two flanking panels of the *Triptych*. The decorative style of the Crivelli brothers (the exuberant ornamentation on the draperies, horse harness and aureols) and the compositional solutions borrowed from Vittore Carpaccio (*St. Martin and the Beggar, St. George Killing the Dragon*) are likewise present, but they only appear as a kind of reminis-

NIKOLA BOŽIDAREVIĆ
Triptych (1517)
Detail.

120

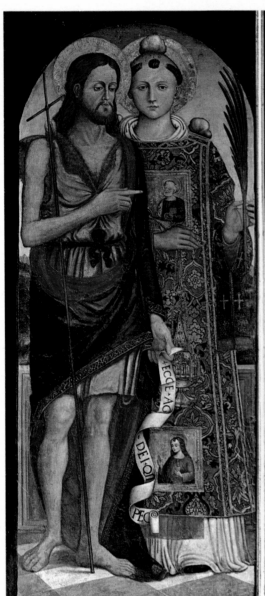

cences from youth, from the time of the artists' first contacts and lessons. However, both in content and figurative expression, the total effect is peculiar only to Dubrovnik and to Božidarević himself. One single theme—communion and the forgiveness of sins—is repeated and developed, as in a skillfully constructed fugue, through all the pictures of the *Triptych*, from the grape and the ear of wheat in the hand of the infant Christ, through the apostles represented on Pope Gregory's cape, and the scene of St. Martin and the beggar, to the Crucifixion in the lunette, with angels collecting Christ's blood into chalices.

MIHOČ HAMZIĆ.   *The Lukarević Triptych.*

Mihoč Hamzić, son of a craftsman from Cologne and pupil of Mantegna, introduced to Dubrovnik and its painting the discipline of his forebears on the Rhine and the rigorously structured forms and cool coloring of his great master Mantegna. This *Triptych* painted for the Lukarević family was created in the late

MIHOČ HAMZIĆ
Ston?–Dubrovnik 1518
The Lukarević Triptych (1513)
Tempera on wood; 76 3/4" x 100"
(Part of the work on the Triptych was done by Hamzić's collaborator, the Venetian painter Pietro di Giovanni).
Dubrovnik, Dominican Church

122

years of the artist's life, and clearly shows that neither the Dalmatian climate, nor the apparent influence of Giovanni Bellini, nor the collaboration with the young Venetian painter Pietro di Giovanni could essentially soften Hamzić's style—basically harsh, voluminous and rationally balanced. In the central panel St. Nicholas is set in a niche like a monumental sculpture, while the two flanking panels (John the Baptist with Stephen the Martyr; and Mary Magdalene with the apostle Mark) are distinguished by their strict isocephalism. The contrasts of light and dark, the deep folds of the draperies and the pronounced drawing stress the sculpturesque form of the figures and the tactile quality of the details, thus typologically linking the entire *Triptych* with Mantegna's "lapidary" style. Only the fragment of deep sky represented in the background of the two side panels shows that Hamzić or his collaborator Pietro di Giovanni were likewise aware of the new currents in Venetian art.

ANDRIJA MEDULIĆ.   *The Legend of Tobias.*
In the Venetian school of the Cinquecento, Andrija Medulić holds a special place. A contemporary of Tintoretto, at times his pupil and at other times his master, and occasionally carried away by the anecdotic scenes of Bonifazio de Pitati, by Parmigiano's etchings and Titian's color, he remained essentially independent, closer to Bassano and El Greco than to his contemporaries. This whimsical artist, about whom even Vasari reluctantly admits that he now and then painted a good picture, decisively did away with balanced Renaissance composition, replaced sharp outlines with a soft sfumato, and thus emerged as one of the founders of Italian Mannerist painting. *The Legend of Tobias,* as illustrated by Medulić, forms a composition in three separate fields, of which the first is dark and cool (Tobias returning home at dusk, with a fish on his shoulders), the second radiant (meeting between son and blind father), and the third all tremulous and warm (preparations for the feast). The dynamic rhythms of movement and light overflow the boundaries suggested by architectural details, so that the individual groups, or rather scenes separated in time and space, are visually experienced as a single whole. Since the painting is illuminated by several sources of light of various positions and unequal strength, the groups seem to be masterfully set like on a movable stage. The colors are denser than Giorgione's, the light effects more dramatic than Titian's, and the rhythms more poetical than Tintoretto's.

ANDRIJA MEDULIĆ
(ANDREA MELDOLA, ANDREA SCIA-
VONE)
Nadin or Zadar, circa 1500–Venice 1563
The Legend of Tobias
Oil on canvas; 11″ x 41″
Zagreb, Strossmayer Gallery

GIOVANNI DA BOLOGNA. *Hercules at Rest.*

At a time when Michelangelo, tormented by thoughts of God and death, sculptured his last, almost dematerialized figures (the *Pietà* in Florence Cathedral, and the *Rondanini Pietà*), a new, fresh force arrived in Rome from the Netherlands: Giovanni da Bologna, then aged twenty-five. The works he produced after 1557 in Florence, under the protection of the Medici family, are representative of Italian sculpture in the transition between the Renaissance and the Baroque. He received his first training in the Flemish town of Mons. Rome perfected his form, but could not essentially change his realistic, Northern vision, while Florence preserved him from the immediate pressure of the Counter-Reformation. His nude figures inspired by classical myths in a Renaissance manner, are endowed with a new sensuousness and solemnity, picturesqueness and dynamic motion. *Hercules at Rest* is a clay model for a large-size sculpture in bronze or marble. The figure conveys an immediate impression, for the Renaissance structure is formally preserved: the composition is simple, the form is seemingly at rest, and the emotion restrained. But the body is not statically set in any spacial context. Though supported in a few places, none of these supports seem stable enough to bear it. The composition lacks horizontals and verticals, symmetry has been abandoned, and the image thus loses any clear points of reference. The artist does not represent the repose of a tired hero, but merely a flighty pause, full of inner restlessness. This hidden tension, bound to the transitory situation, is already a feature of Baroque art.

GIOVANNI DA BOLOGNA
(GIAMBOLOGNA)
Douai 1529–Florence 1608
Hercules at Rest (circa 1563–1567)
Terracotta; 28 3/8"
Zagreb, Strossmayer Gallery
Ante Topić Mimara Collection

VEIT KÖNIGER
Sexten 1720–Graz 1792
The Virgin Mary
Gilt wood carving; 65"
Ljubljana, National Gallery

VEIT KÖNIGER. *The Virgin Mary.* p. 125

Thanks to its compromises between naturalism and idealism, sensuousness and spirituality, the passions of this world and ecstatic piety, Baroque art made a lasting appeal in some regions of Europe. Veit Königer carved his writhing, typically Baroque figures in Graz and Vienna at a time when some other Austrian sculptors had already accepted a new, Neoclassical style. His *Virgin Mary*, small-headed and slender-limbed, completely transported towards heaven and intensely agitated in space, expresses the gracefully shifting equilibrium of late Baroque, its elegant pathos and warm lyricism.

FEDERIKO BENKOVIĆ
Omiš 1677?–Gorica 1753
Sacrifice of Abraham
Oil on canvas; 86 7/8″ x 65″
Zagreb, Strossmayer Gallery

TEODOR KRAČUN
Sremska Kamenica?–Sremski Karlovci 1781
Ascension (1781)
Oil on canvas; 61 1/4″ x 30 1/4″
(From the iconostasis of the Cathedral Church
at Sremski Karlovci).
Belgrade, National Museum

FEDERIKO BENKOVIĆ. *Sacrifice of Abraham.* *p. 126*

The *Sacrifice of Abraham* was long considered a work by Piazzetta, and only in 1935 was it established that this painting was produced by Federiko Benkovic for the castle of Pommersfelden, Germany. The similarity between these two great painters of the Venetian school of the late Baroque period is due to the fact that Benković, just like Piazzetta, formed his style in Bologna, under the strong influence of Giuseppe Maria Crespi. The academicism of Bologna, the tradition of Caravaggio's expressive luminism and the bright Venetian coloring blend in this great picture, to create a vigorous, tragic mood that expresses the drama of sacrificing one's most precious possession to God. The three actors of this drama are unequally illumined. A stream of warm, golden light strikes only the youthful, nude boy of Isaac, the agonized face of Abraham and the uplifted hand of the angel pointing towards heaven, denoting the three highest values, the three kinds of beauty—physical, moral and divine. The picture is composed along diagonal lines intersecting at Isaac's breast, the precise spot toward which the point of the knife is directed, while the light in this area of the painting is arranged in a way that connects the body of the victim with the head of the suffering father, so that Abraham seems to be plunging the blade into his own heart.

TEODOR KRAČUN. *Ascension.* *p. 127*

Two centuries of gradual development in Western European art, from Mannerism to Baroque to Rococo, are telescoped into a single distinctive style in Serbian art between 1770 and 1781, in the work of Teodor Kračun. It is therefore no wonder that art historians have had such diverse opinions as to the sources of Kračun's inspiration: in Byzantine tradition, in Paolo Veronese, El Greco and Tiepolo, in High Renaissance, Mannerism, Baroque and Rococo. It is precisely this escape from any of the usual categories of style that constitutes the chief strength and value of Kračun's painting, in which the Byzantine spirituality, always present beneath the surface, subdues the impetuosity of the Baroque and deepens the flighty moods of Rococo. This is clearly apparent in the *Ascension* of the iconostasis from the Cathedral Church at Sremski Karlovci, in which the vibrant atmosphere of the painting is firmly controlled by the color and the winding forms of the Virgin, and of the Christ above.

HANS GEORG GEIGERFELDER. *St. George Killing the Dragon.* *p. 128*

The dawn of Baroque art in Slovenia is marked by the painting of *St. George Killing the Dragon* from the altar of a chapel near Ortnek Castle, Lower Carniola. The signature "H.G.G." indicates that the author of this dynamic composition is probably Hans Georg Geigerfelder, a painter active in Novo Mesto. Both in its content (the landscape with strewn human bones in the foreground, and a disturbed St. Mary and a castle in the background) and its formal elements (diagonal composition, forthright modelling) this picture is still closely linked to Central European Mannerism; but the bold three-quarter view of the bounding horse, the writhing head of the wounded dragon and the illusionistically deepened space are clear imitations of Baroque.

HANS GEORG GEIGERFELDER
St. George Killing the Dragon (1641), detail
Oil on canvas; 107 1/2" x 59"
(From a chapel near Ortnek Castle in Lower Carniola).
Ljubljana, National Gallery

ADRIAEN VAN OSTADE
Haarlem 1610–1684
Wine Tasting
Oil on canvas; 13 1/4″ x 11 1/8″
Zagreb, Strossmayer Gallery
(Ante Topić Mimara Collection)

ADRIAEN VAN OSTADE.   *Wine Tasting.*

Inspired by the figures of common people in the paintings of his great master Frans Hals, by Brouwer's satirical sketches and by Rembrandt's methods of illumination, Adriaen van Ostade created a series of charming genre scenes, perhaps the finest in all Dutch painting. But *Wine Tasting* lacks the picturesqueness and storytelling capacity characteristic of Adriaen's usual style. The setting in which the good-natured wine expert is depicted is unimaginatively solved: a furtive glimpse into an interior, a grape-trellis, a bird in a cage, and a stereotyped still-life. One can sense that this work was created in the late years of the artist's life, when the painter's passion for observing the events of the outside world has abated, giving way to a sense for expressing psychological responses. The only elements that matter in the picture are the sadness in the wine taster's eyes, and the smile on his lips caused by the sweetness of the sample just tasted.

JOSÉ RIBERA
(LO SPAGNOLETTO)
Játiva near Valencia 1591–Naples 1652
Beggars
Oil on canvas; 57″ x 34 5/8″
Zagreb, Strossmayer Gallery
(Ante Topić Mimara Collection)

130

JOSÉ RIBERA. *Beggars.* p. 131

The bizarre, naturalistic motif of a beggar carrying his crippled colleague in a basket on his back could have become a subject of art only in the country of Cervantes, where madmen, paupers, vagrants, and swashbucklers are often at the same time proud knights and great saints. Ribera probably took this subject from his master Francisco de Ribalta, founder of the naturalist current in Spanish 17th century painting. Neither the lessons received later in Italy (Padua, Parma, Rome), nor his permanent residence in Naples after 1616 could alter Ribera's Spanish temperament, his sense of acute observation, in particular his ability to discover greatness of spirit in the deformed figures of the street. In spite of their abject situation, the two beggars are endowed with mysterious ambiguous eyes—thoughtful and warm, and at the same time sneeringly superior. The stressed theatricalism and the tenebroso manner so typical of Ribera's religious painting are here subdued and replaced by anecdotal objectivity.

JEAN ANTOINE GROS. *Mme. Récamier.* p. 133

Gros painted this *Portrait of Mme. Récamier* after the Restoration of the Bourbon dynasty, possibly in the very same year when his master Jacques Louis David died in exile. Painter and model seem to have found themselves in the same situation and the same mood: the advanced years and the memories of the glory of bygone days cast a slight shadow of sadness on the face of this still beautiful woman, filling her eyes with nostalgia, while the artist's brush dwells on the quiet harmonies of colors, emphasizes the glory of old lace, and stresses the weary hands folded like those of a dead body. The painting sincerely and touchingly describes the psychological drama of two beings frightened by the future, who have shut themselves out from the world and look back sadly on the past. The painter is aware that Géricault has already produced his *Raft of the Medusa* and Delacroix his *Scenes from the Massacre of Chios.* He feels that the new generation has lost touch with his own sense of drawing and color, with the Neoclassical style that had reigned supreme in his youth. In his devotion to David, Gros never realized that it was precisely his own painting—which Elie Faure characterizes as a "tremulous transition between the stability of David and the turmoil of Delacroix"—that inaugurated Romanticism.

DJORDJE KRSTIĆ. *Babakaj.* p. 134

Djordje Krstić's *Babakaj* is a fantastic landscape that sets the vain efforts of man, with his magnificent but perishable monuments, in opposition to the elemental, unceasing forces of nature. The chief masses of the composition are arranged in a diagonal which rises from the group of fishermen working on the bank at lower right, toward the proudly soaring towers of an abandoned castle, up to the monumental rock cliff at left, modelled by storms and the waves of a great river. The gradation of light, however, proceeds in the opposite direction, along another diagonal which rises from the foot of the cliff at left, is lost in the darkness of the troubled river, and rises to the clouds penetrated by the rays of the sun above the fishermen's cottage. The first progression, rational and pragmatic, objectively evaluates man's position in the universe; the second, irrational and visionary, crowns the same tiny beings and its ephemeral works with celestial glamor. Whether these procedures and conceptions are Baroque, Romantic or Realist, *Babakaj* is a stylistically unified, genuine masterpiece.

132

JEAN ANTOINE GROS
Paris 1771–Meudon 1835
Mme. Récamier (circa 1824–25)
Oil on canvas; 24 1/2" x 20 1/8"
Zagreb, Strossmayer Gallery

DJORDJE KRSTIĆ
Stara Kanjiža 1851–Belgrade 1907
Babakaj (1907)
Oil on canvas; 20 5/8″ x 31 1/2″
Belgrade, National Museum

KONSTANTIN DANIL.   *Portrait of the Artist's Wife.*   *p. 135*
The *Portrait of the Artist's Wife* was left unfinished. Not that painter's work
was interrupted by death, but probably by the feeling that any additional brush-
stroke would be redundant, that any further application of paint would deprive
the figure of its reality. Danil, the most remarkable Neoclassical portraitist in
Serbian painting, stopped at the hands: one, drooping wearily with the fingers
hardly indicated, becomes dissolved and almost dematerialized in soft shadow.
The magic of the figure of this mature woman, descended from an impover-
ished Hungarian aristocratic family, reposes precisely on the indefiniteness of
the hands. Because of them, all the lines appear vague, and the basic form loses
definition, making the entire figure look airy and decadently refined. In this
painting Danil's usual Biedermeier naturalism is replaced by romantic sensibility, though this remains restrained, without painful effusions of tenderness.

KONSTANTIN DANIL
Lugoš 1789–Veliki Bečkerek 1873
Portrait of the Artist's Wife (circa 1846)
Oil on canvas; 33 5/8" x 27 3/4"
Belgrade, National Museum

p. 136
CAMILLE COROT
Paris 1796–1875
In the Park (circa 1862)
Oil on canvas; 18 1/2" x 15"
Belgrade, National Museum

CAMILLE COROT.   *In the Park.*   *p. 136*

The landscape with its long shadows, the strange whitish spot in the darkness among the trees, and the human figure seen from afar standing in the sunlit clearing—these are the three elements with which Corot composed his picture *In the Park*. It captures a moment of the late afternoon, shortly before sunset, when silvery tones dissolve sharp contours, and all forms seem to grow, move and revive in the mythical atmosphere of mediation between light and darkness. The woman is set in the center, but is shown only as a part of nature; she swings in the rhythm of the bushes and the trees, while her head is hidden from view, preventing her thoughts and emotions from disturbing the balance achieved. This ideal harmony between man and nature strikes a quiet, solemn chord in the development of French painting of the 19th century. This note was to resound for a long time afterwards in the works of the Impressionists.

135

PART V
MODERN TIMES
(Disintegration of Colors to Novel Forms)

ALFRED SISLEY
Paris 1839–Moret-sur-Loing 1899
Barges on the Loing (1877)
Oil on canvas; 18 1/8" x 15"
Belgrade, National Museum

ALFRED SISLEY.   *Barges on the Loing.*

"Objects must be represented in their interrelations, they must be flooded with light, as they are in nature. . . . The means to achieve this should be the sky." *Barges on the Loing* is a realization of Sisley's meditations on landscape painting. The high blue sky comprises two-thirds of the picture, while the light penetrates through the crowns of the trees, glides down the masts of the barges, plays over the façades of the houses and descends on the quay and the river, creating transparent, flickering shadows along the path, and bright, glimmering reflections on the water. The sky is in no way the background—it is, in fact, the main subject of the painting. Sisley feels that the Impressionist technique of rapid, short brush-strokes is best suited to render the sky, which contains the "charm of everything transitory." Second place is given to the river, but this, too, lacks stability and clarity, firm structure and definite outlines, i.e. all those elements that Impressionist painting resolutely evaded. The reflections on the water are more important than the barges, the trees and the human figures; the surfaces of material objects are more important than their volumes and plastic forms; and the beauty of the momentary situation matters more than any permanent comprehension of nature and man. The financial misery and the painful problems Sisley had to fight following his father's bankruptcy in 1870, did not in the least affect the serenity pervading his *Barges on the Loing*, nor did they dramatically agitate the river.

CAMILLE PISSARRO.   *Square in Front of the Théâtre Français.*   p. 139

After 1886 Pissarro abandoned the spontaneous Impressionist divisionism of color and, under the influence of Seurat, adopted the Neo-Impressionist technique of methodical, rational disintegration of tones; but after a few years he gave up this tiring procedure and with free brush-strokes began painting his glimmering vistas of large modern cities—Paris, Rouen, Le Havre—seen from the height of hotel windows or attic rooms. During his winter sojourns in Paris from 1892 on Pissarro discovered the charm of broad boulevards, the picturesqueness of old façades and the poetry of the sky over a huge city, aglow with a mild, tremulous light. It is precisely this peculiar, indirect illumination, which can neither pale the colors nor dissolve the outlines, that pervades his *Square in Front of the Théâtre Français*: it serves to endow the forms with a golden tone and discreetly soften the contours. The structure of the composition thereby becomes firmer, all the forms assume greater stability, and the cityscape, though on the whole losing some of its lightness, acquires a more definite character. The lively movement in the square, placed within the firm framework of the high façades and dominated by a sky that seems to indicate the approach of spring, suggests the flow of a large river between stony banks. "Everything is beautiful, only one must know how to interpret it," wrote Pissarro in 1893.

EDGAR DEGAS.   *Ballerinas in Blue.*   p. 140

Ballerinas in Blue possesses the essential strength of Degas' style: the objective, incisive rendering of form and motion by means of rudimentary outlines and harmoniously blending colors. It is a study of arm movement which not only fixes and congeals a momentary action, but above all emphasizes the beauty of an unbroken arabesque, intensely agitated, but perfectly balanced.

The ballerina in the center, represented obliquely, is caught in a highly unstable pose, but is firmly flanked by the figures of her two partners, one of whom is

leaning back with head uplifted, while the other is bending forward. Their arms, arranged in contrary directions, form a solid frame for the central figure, and at the same time determine the structure of the entire composition. By this procedure Degas demonstrates that even while representing a momentary gesture it is possible to create coherent forms with a feeling of permanence.

CAMILLE PISSARRO
Saint-Thomas 1830–Paris 1903
Square in Front of the Théâtre Français (1898)
Oil on canvas; 29 1/2" x 37"
Belgrade, National Museum

139

AUGUSTE RENOIR. *Girl with a Straw Hat.*   *p. 141*

The *Girl with a Straw Hat* typifies the exuberance and youthful freshness of Renoir's entire oeuvre; its manner and style are characteristic of that important stage in his work when his plastic forms bathed in full light seem to coalesce organically with the atmosphere. The girl, in a dress of violent red and with attention absorbed in her large straw hat, seems like a synthesis of the spring and summer of life, of the warm yellow of blossoming sunflowers and the golden glow of ripe wheat. The outlines are far from definite, but the form is by no means dissolved into space—it remains solid and massive. Though the light is bright, the colors do not disintegrate: they flare in the light and interpenetrate freely in mild half-tones. Renoir did not arrive at these results immediately and without pain. From 1883 to 1890, inspired by the classicist draftmanship of Renaissance models, he endeavored to reinstate definition and firmness of form, though at the same time treating colors like a Manet or Monet. Only after he had resolutely broken with the past, was Renoir able to penetrate into the very substance of matter and to realize, aided by his richness of tones, the long-desired balance between firmness of continuous form and softness of diffuse light. The figure of the girl is modelled on this new principle of colorist plasticity, while the tones of blue, grey, brown and green of the background project a soft, velvety glow—the glow that shimmers from almost all of Renoir's paintings after 1890.

EDGAR DEGAS
Paris 1834–1917
Ballerinas in Blue (circa 1900)
Pastel and charcoal on paper; 16″ x 24 3/4″
Belgrade, National Museum

AUGUSTE RENOIR
Limoges 1841–Cagnes 1919
Girl with a Straw Hat (circa 1895)
Pastel on paper; 24″ x 18 1/2″
Belgrade, National Museum

MAURICE UTRILLO. *Rue Mont-Cenis.*

Rue Mont-Cenis is one of Utrillo's numerous "dialogues" with the city, the suburbs of Paris and their modest whitewashed houses, steep stairs, sidewalks and rare passers-by. What surprises in this "dialogue" is Utrillo's timid evasion of man. The artist assigns the principal roles to the street-lamp, the dilapidated wall, the tall chimneys and the buildings themselves, whose open windows seem to resemble huge, empty eyes. What does the wall in the foreground or the high attic in the background hide? This remains a mystery, for Utrillo, with his quiet outlines and unobtrusive colors, only describes the outside appearance of simple façades, behind which the most varied dramas of life may be taking place. One cannot escape the feeling that the artist deliberately evades these, for he represents his street early in the morning, when everything seems to be breathing deeply and quietly. Not even have the customs-officer Rousseau and the naïve painters of the 20th century been able so movingly to define the line that separates man from inert matter.

MAURICE UTRILLO
Paris 1883–Dax 1955
Rue Mont-Cenis (circa 1929)
Oil on canvas; 18 1/4" x 21 5/8"
Belgrade, National Museum

142

PAUL GAUGUIN. *Tahitian Woman.*

"In this simple, naked parable I wished to invoke a certain ancient, barbarian splendor. It is all concentrated in the colors, which are intentionally dark and gloomy; the splendor is not in silk, nor velvet, nor fine cloth, nor gold, but in the texture of the body itself, heightened by the artist's hand. There is no trick . . . it is human imagination itself, with its power of vision, that has enriched this world." These words from a letter that Gauguin wrote in 1897 to his friend Daniel de Monfreid seem to describe the *Tahitian Woman* in the Belgrade National Museum. Gauguin had already represented a nude female figure in almost the same pose in 1897, and he was to render it once again in his great composition *Where do we come from? What are we? Where are we going?.*

It is difficult to discover at first sight what is new and important in this "naked parable." But from this composition have been eliminated all those details with which Gauguin, in the first years of his stay on Tahiti, liked to stress the charms of this "fragrant isle." The painting is dominated by the nude figure, set in front of an indefinite tangle of vegetation and an empty boat on a river. Both the pose of the figure and the colors suggest a strange apathy, a tense expectation of something malignant and mysterious in the stifling atmosphere and complete solitude of the wilderness. This may be a presage of death, or that "holy terror" mentioned in Gauguin's letters of 1897 and 1898.

PAUL GAUGUIN
Paris 1848–La Dominique 1903
Tahitian Woman (1898)
Oil on canvas; 36 3/4" x 51 1/8"
Belgrade, National Museum

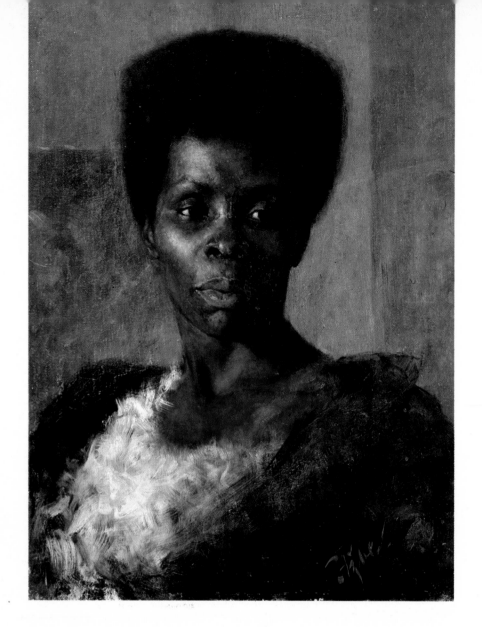

ANTON AŽBE
Dolenjčice near Škofja Loka 1862–Munich 1905
Negro Woman (1895)
Oil on canvas; 21 3/4" x 15 1/2"
Ljubljana, National Gallery

ANTON AŽBE. *Negro Woman.*

Anton Ažbe was both an avant-garde teacher and a conservative painter. From 1891 on in his famous school of painting in Munich he taught theories of form ("the spheric principle") and color ("cristallization of colors") that were close to Cézanne's and Manet's ideas. But while his numerous pupils, on return to their respective native countries, became leaders of modern painting there (Jakopic, Grohar, Sternen and Jama in Slovenia, Račić and Becić in Croatia, Nadežda Petrović in Serbia), and even the creators of the most extreme forms of expression (Kandinsky), Ažbe's own paintings remain, on the whole, faithful to the tenets of Munich realism.

The portrait of the *Negro Woman* only in part explains Ažbe's theoretical principles. The head is firmly, almost cubically modelled, and the clear, transparent colors reflect something of that "diamond radiance" towards which Ažbe strove; but the total effect lags far behind the author's bold teachings.

NADEŽDA PETROVIĆ. *Resnik.* p. 145

On the rustic path leading to a remote Serbian village, Nadežda Petrović created her *Resnik*—this bold, passionate painting, with its violent applications of

NADEŽDA PETROVIC
Čačak 1873–Valjevo 1915
Resnik (circa 1904)
Oil on canvas; 27 1/2″ x 38 1/2″
Belgrade, National Museum

glaring colors and angular, dramatically broken brushstrokes—possibly in the very same year that Expressionism was formulated in Dresden (the *Brücke* movement) and Fauvism hatched in Paris (Autumn Salon of 1905).

At that moment, far from any contacts with the latest currents rising in the great artistic centers—her painter's education having been obtained at first in Belgrade, in the studio of Djordje Krstić, and later in Munich, in Anton Ažbe's school—she discovered, by the mere impulse of her temperament, new expressive values of color. According all priority to subjective observation, she outgrew Impressionism, replacing its hedonism with ardent social engagement.

MIROSLAV KRALJEVIĆ. *Luxembourg Park*   p. 146

Moving from Zagreb to Munich to Paris, i.e. through the Croatian cultural influences of Jugendstil and Impressionism, Kraljevic evolved his own personal artistic expression, which between 1906 and 1913 developed from tonal painting through Manet's discoveries to Cézanne's constructivism.

Luxembourg Park, all in cool green tones, painted with dynamic brushstrokes and impasto surfaces, is quite unusually composed. In the center of the canvas

there is an empty shady space, framed by the trees and the bench on which three women are sitting with their faces turned towards the vague, but intensely lighted area in the background. The tree-trunks and their crowns are arranged in such a way that the space in the foreground is transformed into a firm, closed cube, whose emptiness, or rather the mysterious something it hides, is stressed as the main content of the painting. Kraljević in this painting lays down the "motif" as understood by Cézanne.

MIROSLAV KRALJEVIĆ
Gospić 1885–Zagreb 1913
Luxembourg Park (1912)
Oil on canvas; 21 1/4″ x 25 1/8″
Zagreb, Modern Gallery

JOSIP RAČIĆ.   *Portrait of a Lady in Black.*   p. 147

It is difficult to connect the *Portrait of a Lady in Black* with any special stylistic tendency. Račić, whose entire painter's work was limited to a period of only four years (1904-1908), cannot be said to have adopted either Secessionist leanings, or the tenets of Impressionism; yet in his rapid surge towards maturity he formulated a personal style that can be defined as "sensitive neorealism."

The *Lady in Black* only superficially, by her pose and costume, conveys some of the decadent feeling characteristic of the "*fin de siècle.*" In its morphology and refined use of color this portrait is, first of all, linked to Leibl and Manet, and through them to the old masters, like Holbein and Vermeer, Goya and Velasquez. These are, however, mere affinities and by no means influences that can deprive Račić's painting of its originality and call it anachronistic. The summary color scale and the simple, firmly modelled form of the *Lady in Black* correspond perfectly with modern sensibility.

JOSIP RAČIĆ
Zagreb 1885–Paris 1908
Portrait of a Lady in Black (1907)
Oil on canvas; 37 5/8″ x 27 3/4″
Zagreb, Modern Gallery

RIHARD JAKOPIĆ. *Shoal.*

The painting of Rihard Jakopić is a proof that Impressionism, in its triumphal conquest of Europe, met the same fate as earlier international styles. In a new environment—in this case on the territory of Slovenia—French Impressionism merely played the role of catalizer, causing an upheaval in the local cultural tradition and influencing the formation of a highly original expression.

Jakopić's *Shoal* resumes the specific atmosphere of the Slovenian landscape and presents, moreover, a totally new expression of the outside world. It is figuratively closer to the restless colorist abstractions of August Giacometti than to the passive, essentially naturalistic descriptions of light and nature of a Monet or a Sisley.

HENRI MATISSE. *At the Window.*   *p. 149*

The open window is a frequent subject in Matisse's painting: it gives him the opportunity of ideally combining the interior, the human figure and the outdoors. In this process Matisse abolishes perspective, neglects the third dimension, and sets the three heterogeneous elements practically on the same plane. The human figure is what interests the artist most, for through it he can express his "almost religious sense of life."

In this painting the young woman is shown from the back, but the calligraphic arabesque of her crossed hands and her hidden face clearly enough describe a mood of quiet contemplation in a dignified environment. The colors are chosen in accordance with that mood; without shadows or half-tones, they are fastidiously applied to the flat surfaces that construct the picture in magic harmony.

RIHARD JAKOPIČ
Ljubljana 1869–1943
Shoal (1919)
Oil painting on canvas; 46 1/2″ x 54″
Ljubljana, Modern Gallery

HENRI MATISSE
Le Cateau–Cambrésis 1869–Nice 1954
At the Window (circa 1918)
Oil on canvas; 28 3/4″ x 23 5/8″
Belgrade, National Museum

NEDELJKO GVOZDENOVIĆ. *Park.*
In the bewildering succession of modern art movements certain signs of a return to peace and order have always been apparent. In Serbian painting this
tendency is linked to the vision of Nedeljko Gvozdenović, whose *Park*
reaffirms the belief in the possibility of establishing genuine contacts between
man and the world, in the redeeming powers of reason and goodness. The actual representation of the trees, meadows, sculptures and passers-by of a small
city park is in no way the essential subject of this picture; the real content is the
tracery of silvery curves formed by the gravelly paths, which intersect and outline the green surfaces crossed by the dim verticals of plants and trees. To
make this abstract arabesque even clearer and more impressive, the color scale
is simplified to a minimum. *Park* demonstrates that there is no real antagonism
between figurative and abstract art.

MARKO ČELEBONOVIĆ. *Interior with Figure and Plaster Head.*   p. 151
The inner dialogue of man with inanimate objects and with the past is the theme
of Čelebonović's painting *Interior with Figure and Plaster Head.* On one side
we see a man lost in thought and flowers in a vase, on the other side a plaster
head and a potted plant stunted in the suffocating atmosphere of a closed room.
In the background, but clearly in a central position, is an empty arm-chair, evidently a reminder of some absent being who once played an important part in

NEDELJKO GVOZDENOVIĆ
Mostar 1902
Park (1951)
Oil on canvas; 26″ x 39 3/8″
Belgrade, National Museum

150

MARKO ČELEBONOVIĆ
Belgrade, 1902
Interior with Figure and Plaster Head (1937)
Oil on canvas; 70 7/8" x 63"
Belgrade, Museum of Contemporary Art

this environment. The restricted color scale, in which greens and greyish ochre predominate, adds a note of coolness to this melancholy, pent-up world, in which everything has stopped—a world without sound, without movement, without a future. The numerous objects seem to be defending the figure from solitude and from the anxiety of universal transitoriness. It is the atmosphere of Marcel Proust, a painter's interpretation of the search for time lost.

MILO MILUNOVIĆ. *Fish-Trap.*
This work epitomises the essential traits of Milunović's distinctively cerebral painting, which never swerved from its straight filiation: Byzantine fresco; Early Renaissance; Poussin; Cézanne; Braque. The dense weave of a fish trap is an ideal theme for an artist who always strove to confine organic forms in a network of horizontals and verticals, to represent them as definite, static and rationally comprehensible. Therefore his subject assumes the value of a symbol of the principle underlying Milunović's art, expressing with its boldly drawn lines, its stable architectonics and its restrained color the artist's firm belief that everything that is valuable and beautiful is contained in intellectual reasoning, in measure, restraint, proportion and balance. The colors, which conjure up a Mediterranean climate, are linked to Milutinović's heliotropism, his Apollonian view of the world, and his need for silence, even at the expense of personal suffering and the risk of his own inadequacy as a painter—that other voice ever-present in man reminding him of the evanescence of his sunshine existence and the inevitable return of all things into primordial darkness.

152

MILO MILUNOVIĆ
Cetinje 1897–Belgrade 1967
Fish-Trap
Oil on canvas; 33″ x 51 1/8″
Belgrade, Museum of Contemporary art

PETAR LUBARDA. *Horses.*

Petar Lubarda's *Horses* represents the stormy conflict between two colors, the dramatic fight between a light and a dark arabesque, the mythic battle between day and night, good and evil, life and death—the psychological struggle between the conscious and the subconscious, the rational and the irrational. The powers of darkness are doubled, but the force of light is stronger, so the outcome of the fight remains uncertain. The strong rhythm of heavy, but free outlines, surfaces activated by contrasts between pure colors and tones, unreal depthless space—these are the only means suitable to the figurative embodiment of this modern mythic vision. It is necessary only to recall the horse from the eastern frieze of the Parthenon—that placid, idyllic depiction of the myth of the reconciliation between day and night, that long-cherished dream of the ancient Greeks. Lubarda has no need for such self-deception. He is endowed with the force of a highland peasant and the sensibility of a cosmopolitan, gifts that embolden him to transpose the truth about life into allegory: the constant struggle of two equivalent energies in diametrically opposed movements.

PETAR LUBARDA
Ljubotin 1907
Horses (1953)
Oil on canvas; 57 7/8″ x 72 7/8″
Belgrade, Museum of Contemporary Art

153

KRSTO HEGEDUŠIĆ. *Dead Waters.*

Early in life deeply affected by the tragedy of his native land, by the misery of
the Podravina peasants. Hegedušić in the period after the Second World War
suffered from the painful pressures of cosmic absurdity. From an emotive realist of the stamp of a Pieter Brueghel, he developed into a vehement Surrealist,
an interpreter of general existential anguish. *Dead Waters* is a painting which in
its composition, its atmosphere and its content recalls the modern "theatre of
the absurd," the heavy and complex constructions of a Beckett or a Ionesco.
The picture is a collection of symbols with negative meanings, all implying an
oppressive nightmare, foreboding a cosmic cataclysm. The composition is
dominated by horizontals, indicating a general stagnation and the approaching
end of the world. The verticals are all short, hesitant and directed into empty
space—as if reaching for life, thought, hope. The deformed bodies of the
drowned, the face with the glazed pupils turned towards the pitiless sky, the
empty dock, the uprooted tree-stumps and leafless branches create the sense of

KRSTO HEGEDUSIC
Petrinja 1901
Dead Waters (1956)
Tempera and oil on canvas; 51 1/8″ x 63 3/4″
Belgrade, Museum of Contemporary Art

IVAN GENERALIĆ
Hlebine 1914
The Woodcutters (1959)
Oil painting on glass; 28″ x 47 5/8″
Zagreb, Gallery of Primitive Art

a devastating catastrophe, a shocking vision of the final days of humanity. The entire organic world dissolves in poisonous, leaden water. Hegedušić transcends his presentiment about the future, his fear of an atomic war, and projects into his forms—upturned in the pale light and polluted air—an intimation of a solution of the conflict between the drive for life and the drive for death. He suggests the subconscious yearning of all beings for an absolute equilibrium, a return into non-being, into the eternal peace of the inorganic world.

IVAN GENERALIĆ.   *The Woodcutters.*

To appreciate the value of *The Woodcutters*, it is not absolutely necessary to know that Ivan Generalic lives in a village, that he is self-taught, and is the chief representative of the peasant-painters of Hlebine. The picture is a fairy tale in green and blue, with a peacock among the trees with cut branches and the busy peasants—both in its form and in its content the work of an inspired, great artist. There is nothing "naïve" or "primitive" here: The green of the grass and the blue tones of the sky constrict the black of the bare tree-trunks to isolated narrow strips, presaging the glamor of the approaching spring. The human figures are arranged in two parallel zones, the frieze of the earth and the frieze of the sky, and face in opposite directions: the women, with dead branches in their hands, are turned towards the warmth of home and the fireplace, towards winter and the present, while the men, with their axes, whose strokes will promote the growth of new shoots, are looking towards the peacock, towards spring and the future. Generalić has painted a parable of the oppositions of the seasons, and of the oppositions between the sexes.

DIMITAR KONDOVSKI
Prilep 1927
Polyptych (1963)
Tempera and gold on panel; 48″ x 33″
Skopje, Museum of Contemporary Art

DIMITAR KONDOVSKI. *Polyptych.*

Kondovski began his painting activity with figuration inspired by Modigliani, the early Picasso and the medieval icon painters. Gradually, his link to the native tradition, to the indigenous art of Macedonia, has become increasingly apparent, though not in a formal sense. In his latest stage, Kondovski reaches to the deepest roots of his national culture. Nourished by its vital sap he creates forms hitherto unseen, which can be defined as "non-figurative icons."

His *Polyptych* is carried out in the meticulous technique of the medieval "zoographers," but filled with modern sensibility and cosmopolitan content. This

MARIJ PREGELJ
Kranj 1913–Ljubljana 1967
Fantastic Feast (1966)
Oil on canvas; 69 1/4″ x 58 7/8″
Belgrade, Museum of Contemporary Art

painting seems to offer a solution to the ancient conflict between the iconophiles and iconoclasts, of the age-old clash between the religious, philosophical and esthetic conceptions of West and East, Europe and Asia. Kondovski is an iconoclast in love with icons. Therefore his *Polyptych*, too, is ambivalent. The size, color and feeling of this painting suggest the icons of the Orthodox church, while the forms represented are linked to symbols of the iconoclastic Jewish and Moslem worlds.

MARIJ PREGELJ. *Fantastic Feast.*
In this painting Pregelj represents the brutal ritual enacted unceasingly on the blood-stained table of life; he has succeeded in this by means of an entirely original artistic formula forged from neoexpressionist figuration containing reminiscences of "informal" art, and the experiments of the late Picasso and Henry Moore. An emphatic horizontal separates crude matter from organic bodies, half-defined, still in their formative stage, hesitating, bound to the flesh and blood of their substrata and simultaneously striving towards light and intelligence, which can be vaguely surmised in the grey background above. From   **157**

the egg, that symbol of primordial creation, the most varied forms emerge, monstrous beings endowed with voracious jaws and greedy eyes. Worn out by their mutual struggle, they disintegrate and die even before acquiring a rational shape. There is no real difference between the simplest and the most complicated of these organisms. Both the amoeba and *homo sapiens* crawl under the sun, behave in the same way and share the same fate. Unable to outgrow their biological origins, but nevertheless attracted to the light, they writhe painfully along their short life spans. The imperatives of instinct and of the body are stronger than those of will and spirit.

VJENCESLAV RICHTER.   *Vertical Rhythms.*

Vjenceslav Richter, architect by education and profession, affirms in this sculpture the clearly defined surfaces and pure volumes that Le Corbusier considered to be in accordance with the cosmic order and to represent the basic elements of the architecture of the future. From the multitude of geometric forms, Richter has chosen the rectangle, and by multiplying this unit has created a "systematic sculpture." This constitutes, in fact, a kind of ideal architecture, entirely liberated from submission to material requirements. The forms obtained in this way reflect the microcosm and macrocosm of the artist and his time: the numerous, varied structures of the modern city and the world.

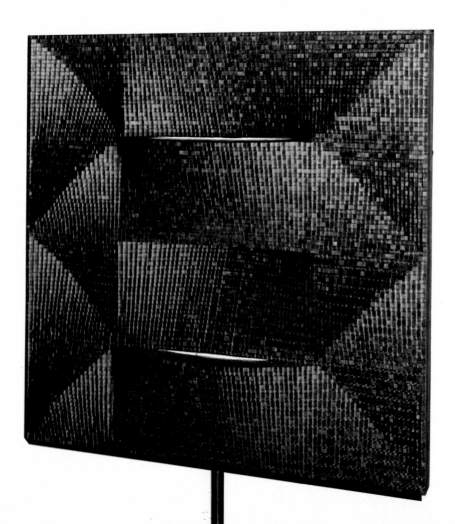

VJENCESLAV RICHTER
Zagreb 1917
Vertical Rhythms (1968)
Aluminum; 23 5/8″ x 23 5/8″ x 11 3/4″
Zagreb, Gallery of Contemporary Art

158

GABRIJEL STUPICA
Dražgoše 1913
Girl with Toys (1956)
Tempera on canvas; 29 1/2″ x 45 1/4″
Ljubljana, Modern Gallery

p. 160
VASA-VELIZAR MIHIĆ
Otočac 1933
Bouquet (1970)
Plexiglas with color; 4″ x 4″ x 35 1/2″
Belgrade, Museum of Contemporary Art

GABRIJEL STUPICA.   *Girl with Toys.*

The attributes of things and beings, their essence and their mutual situation in space are the main theme of this painting. The toys arranged on a dark table and the little girl with outstretched hands are set in a gloomy, indefinite place; with bright, carefully chosen colors all the forms are clearly defined and their independence stressed. By this treatment the toys are transmuted into luminous bodies, close together in space, but nevertheless strictly isolated one from another. Likewise the girl is separated from her toys: any spiritual link is lacking. The girl is uninterested in the things spread on the table, and her attention is engaged in another direction. She is apparently the mistress of the toys, but her ownership over them liberates her from them. Only in Velasquez's portraits of infantas are children equated to such an extent with adults and represented as mysteriously superior to the surrounding objects.

VASA-VELIZAR MIHIĆ.   *Bouquet.*   *p. 160*

The basic aspiration of modern sculpture—the harmonious fusion of sculptural elements with pictorial, luminous and spacial effects—is successfully realized in Mihić's *Bouquet.* Four cubes are arranged to create a multitude of sharply defined planes that permit a violent color orchestration without affecting the volume of the construction or its relation to space. This cubical inclosure, this absence of any imprecision of form, the subordination to crystal-like geometric structure is a tendency common to the sculpture of the ancient Orient, archaic Greece and the modern world.

HISTORY AND DIRECTORY
OF YUGOSLAVIAN MUSEUMS

MUSEUMS OF YUGOSLAVIA (HISTORICAL SURVEY)

The short history of Yugoslav museums reflects the hard political destiny of the Yugoslav nations in the past, while their exceptionally rich collections reflect the strong cultural traditions of their territory. These collections display, above all, the deep cultural roots of the central and western sections of the Balkans, and the creative energies of the Yugoslav nations themselves, whose highest achievements have always been the fruit of their own soil. Therefore the museums of Yugoslavia are distinguished by a character quite their own, and their atmosphere has been preserved pure, distinctive and intimate.

The museums of the world have not coincided with periods of the cultural development and bloom of their respective nations, but rather grown in times of economic and political prosperity, that is to say at a time when they have been able to share the benefits of world civilization. The exceptionally unfavorable historic situation of southwestern Europe from the 14th to the 19th centuries considerably retarded that moment on the territories that were to constitute Yugoslavia. Therefore, in spite of the intense flourishing of culture in the past, the museums of Yugoslavia were founded with a delay of almost a century after other European museums.

Actually, the seeds of Yugoslav museums were sown in the 15th century, roughly at the same time as the first galleries of antiquities, collections of paintings and cabinets of rarities began to appear in other parts of Europe. But while out of these modest beginnings great galleries and museums sprang up in Italy, France, Spain and England in the succeeding centuries, the Yugoslav territories experienced a long period of suppression of national rights and the destruction or impoverishment of all places where culture was cherished: towns, castles, monasteries and churches. Up to the 19th century, small collections of armor, engravings, paintings or ancient coins were only sporadically established in various localities, but their existence was bound to be short-lived, and their importance is now historical rather than cultural and artistic. For a long time the free city of Dubrovnik took the lead in these endeavors to preserve the cultural heritage of the past. In the 16th century, under the influence of Renaissance ideas, her dukes and noblemen began collecting antiquities and paintings of native and foreign masters, and in the 17th century men like Kristifor Stojković and Djoro Baglivi possessed large numismatic collections and cabinets of antiquities. During the same period important collections of Greek and Roman coins also existed in the other large coastal towns, and there was even a kind of antique sculpture gallery: the humanist Dinko Papalić, aided by Marko Marulić, collected classical inscriptions from Salona and built them into the atrium of his palace in Split; while in Northern Croatia count Nikola Drašković and his stepson assembled a rich numismatic collection, which they sold to Emperor Leopold in 1690. Another famous collection was that of the counts Zrinjski in Čakovec, which as early as 1660 included, besides ancient coins and arms, a gallery of paintings and sculptures. In Slovenia, all the great noblemen of the 17th century established cabinets of curiosities in their castles (Križ, Ptuj, Dol near Ljubljana) and—of particular interest—the historian J. V. Valvasor (1614–93) arranged the first organized collection in his castle of Bogensperk, which can be considered the country's first private museum, for it contained, among other valuable objects, no less than 10,000 prints. His Croatian imitators were Pavo Riter Vitezović, and Ican Aletin, a citizen of Dubrovnik: Vitezović kept a small museum in his Zagreb house about 1693 (it was destroyed by fire in 1706),while Aletin systematically arranged his valuable collections according to scientific disciplines. In Serbia, Macedonia, Montenegro and Bosnia-Herzegovina the conditions were not yet ripe for such cultural activity, because of the highly oppressive Turkish administration. The enslaved nations of these regions could find some consolation only in the "museums" already existing, created as a matter of course: the monasteries of the 12th to 14th centuries, still intact, and constituting veritable galleries of their saints, rulers and martyrs, in their way unique in the world.

Because of the increasing pressure of Turkish administration in the eastern regions and the Hapsburg monarchy in the west, museum activity died out throughout the Yugoslav territories in the 18th century. Except for the *Archiepiscopal Museum of Split (Museum spalatinum archiepiscopale),* founded in 1750, this period is marked only by the rummaging of some isolated passionate collectors of antiquities on the sites of the ancient cities of Mursa, Salona, Siscia and Sirmium. While in Western Europe this was the century that saw the establishment of today's leading museums of the world—the *British Museum* (1753) and the *Louvre* (opened to the public in 1746 and 1750)—all the forces of the Yugoslav nations were engaged in the affirmation of their national rights and their preparations for the wars of liberation in the following century. Only the 19th century, simultaneously with the outbreak of the liberation movement, witnessed the formation of the first museums on Yugoslav territory in the modern sense of the word. By 1850 museums had been founded in Split (1818), Ljubljana (1821), Zadar (1830), Zagreb (1836), Belgrade (1843) and Novi Sad (1847). But while during this period, thanks to the Napoleonic wars, precious monuments from Egypt, Greece and other ancient countries were accruing to the *Louvre,* the *British Museum* and the *Hermitage,* the first Yugoslav museums only collected materials from their own regions. They were enriched by what was found in the ruins of Salona and of Diocletian's Palace, on the Adriatic islands, on the sites of Emona, Siscia or Sirmium, on the territory of Belgrade itself, on the wide plains of Vojvodina or in liberated Serbia. Between 1850 and the First World War the existing museum collections were further extended and organized with astonishing rapidity, and some new museums were founded, often with highly specialized collections. Some of the towns that obtained their museums during that time were: Dubrovnik (1872), Osijek (1877), Vršac (1882), Sarajevo (1888), Cetinje (1893) and Pula (1902). A *Museum of Croatian Antiquities* was founded in Knin (1893); and the *Strossmayer Gallery* (opened in 1884), the *Modern Gallery* (1909) and the *Cabinet of Graphics* (1916) were established in Zagreb. Thus a relatively dense net of museums covered almost all Yugoslav regions, while some of the collections now included important works of foreign masters (in the *Strossmayer Gallery* a number of highly valuable paintings of the Italian masters of the 14th–17th centuries; and the *Cabinet of Graphics* some prints by Dürer and Callot).

This exuberant growth of museums on Yugoslav territory was brutally cut by the First World War. Between 1914 and 1918 numerous treasures were lost forever, and the majority of museum collections were ravaged. After the war, in the then united country, all the museums were re-established, but their further development was uneven. In Belgrade the *National Museum* was rebaptized the *Museum of History and Art* (1930), and later named *Prince Paul Museum* (1936); it was rapidly enriched with the materials found in the excavations of Vinča, Starčevo, Pločnik and Stobi, with paintings of Italian, Dutch and French masters of the 17th and 18th centuries, and by an important collection of French painting (Corot, Gauguin, Renoir, Degas). Zagreb was granted a *Collection of Plaster Casts* (1937), in Split an *Artists' Gallery* (1931) was established, in Ljubljana a *National Gallery* (1933) and a *City Museum* (1935), and in Skopje a *Museum of Southern Serbia* (1921). Other museums, too, expanded or reorganized their collections, but to a considerably smaller extent. Only after the Second World War, thanks to a Museum Bill and to the organized service of protection of cultural monuments, the museums of Yugoslavia began to develop their activities systematically. They were reorganized, radically rearranged, and to a great extent transformed into scientific institutions with their exhibits disposed according to the most up-to-date museological principles. In addition to numerous local museums, the newly founded institutions of national character that certainly deserve mentioning are the *Modern Gallery* in Ljubljana (1947), the *Gallery of Primitive Art* (1952) and *Gallery of Contemporary Art* (1955) in Zagreb, the *Meštrović Gallery* in Split (1952), the *Fresco Gallery* (1953) and *Museum of Contemporary Art* (1958) in Belgrade, the *Museum of Vojvodina* (1947) and *Gallery of the Matica Srpska* (1958) in Novi Sad, the *Gallery of Art* in Sarajevo (1947) and the *Archaeological Museum* in Skopje (1949). In the postwar period, an ever greater number of museums lost their local or regional character and outgrew their traditions. Among their new acquisitions special prominence is given to items that can endow the respective museum with an atmosphere of "international synthesis." Some Yugoslav museums possess, in fact, exhibits that are, in their way, unique in the world: the monumental stone sculptures from Lepenski Vir (*Archaeological Collection of the University*, Belgrade), neolithic anthropomorphous figurines (*National Museum*, Belgrade; *Museum of Kosovo and Metohija*, Prishtina; *Regional Museum*, Sarajevo; and *National Museum*, Bitola), the achievements of Veneto-Illyrian metalwork (*National Museum*, Ljubljana; and *Regional Museum*, Sarajevo), icons and frescoes of the 12th–14th centuries (*Museum of Icons*, Ochrid; and *Fresco Gallery*, Belgrade), medieval tombstones, the "stećaks" (*Regional Museum*, Sarajevo), and the creations of the naïve painters (*Gallery of Primitive Art*, Zagreb). Today, Yugoslavia boasts of more than two hundred museums, galleries and special collections, whose teams of experts, organized contacts with the public and valuable exhibitions have assured them a respectable place in the great family of the museums of the world.

Belgrade

National Museum (Narodni muzej)

The museum was founded in 1844. The permanent exhibition shows chiefly materials from Serbia, from the earliest times to the 16th century, as well as works of art, both Yugoslav and foreign, from the 16th century to the Second World War. The museum boasts a rich fund of items from the prehistoric, ancient and early medieval periods, an exceptionally valuable numismatic collection, and a valuable collection of icons and medieval jewellery. The Gallery of Native Art possesses the most complete collection of Serbian art of the 18th–20th centuries and some representative sculptures of Ivan Meštrović, while the Gallery of Foreign Art houses important works of Italian and Flemish masters and a particularly precious collection of French Impressionists, notably Renoir and Degas.

Museum of the Serbian Orthodox Church (Muzej srpske pravoslavne crkve)

The museum was founded in 1936, but has only been open to visitors since 1954. It possesses a rich collection of objects of church art, mostly from the monasteries of Fruška Gora and the churches of eastern Srem (unique collection of ancient textiles, icons, portraits of church notables, sacred objects, rare prints).

Fresco Gallery (Galerija fresaka)

The gallery was founded in 1953. It contains copies of the most important achievements of Yugoslav medieval painting and sculpture. The permanent exhibition gives a cross-section of Yugoslav medieval art from the stylistic, chronological and territorial viewpoints.

Archaeological Collection of the University (Arheološka zbirka Univerziteta)

The collection was established in 1929. Its basic fund is formed by the materials from the huge prehistoric settlement discovered in Vinča near Belgrade. After the last war the collection was augmented with the inclusion of archaeological materials from Židovar (Bronze and Iron Ages) and Lepenski Vir (Mesolithic, Early Neolithic).

Museum of Contemporary Art (Musej savremene umetnosti)

The museum was founded in 1958. Its permanent exhibition shows masterpieces of Yugoslav art of the 20th century.

Zagreb

Archaeological Museum (Arheološki musej)

The museum was founded in 1846. It contains extensive collections of materials from the Prehistoric, ancient and early medieval periods, a large numismatic collection and a collection of Egyptian and Etrurian antiquities (including the longest known Etrurian inscription).

Strossmayer Gallery of Ancient Masters (Strossmayerova galerija starih majstora), belonging to the Yugoslav Academy of Sciences and Arts

The gallery was established and opened to the public in 1884. Its basic holdings consist of the private collection of Bishop Josip Juraj Strossmayer. In the course of time it has been complemented by the collections of numerous donors (in particular those of Étienne de Piennes and of Anti Tipić Mimara) and other acquisitions. The gallery is today the most representative exhibition of old masters on Yugoslav territory. On permanent display are works of the Italian schools of the 14th–18th centuries, of Dutch, Flemish and Central European masters of the 15th–17th centuries and French masters of the 18th–19th centuries.

Modern Gallery (Moderna galerija), belonging to the Institute of Plastic Arts of the Yugoslav Academy of Sciences and Arts
The gallery was established in 1934, and has been administered by the Yugoslav Academy since 1947. Its permanent exhibition represents all currents of Croatian art of the 19th and 20th centuries.

Gallery of Primitive Art (Galerija primitivne umjetnosti)
The gallery was founded in 1952. The permanent exhibition shows paintings and sculptures of Yugoslav naïve painters, the so-called "naïves."

Ljubljana

National Museum (Narodni muzej)
The history of the museum begins in 1821, but it was only opened to the public at large in 1888. The basic collection is represented by the archaeological materials from the numerous prehistoric, ancient and early medieval sites of Slovenia. The museum also includes a rich cabinet of ancient coins and prints.

National Gallery (Narodna galerija)
The gallery was opened to the public in 1919, but obtained its present building and organization in 1933. It possesses rich collections of works of art, originating mostly from the territory of Slovenia, ranging from the 13th century up to 1930.

Modern Gallery (Moderna galerija)
This gallery was established in 1948. Its permanent exhibition shows masterpieces of Slovenian artists from Impressionism to our day.

Zadar

Archaeological Museum (Arheološki muzej)
The museum was established in 1830. Its basic holdings consist of archeological materials from the Iron Age necropoles and ancient settlements of

Dalmatia. There is also a rich collection of pre-Romanesque sculpture. The permanent exhibition gives a cross-section of the culture of northern Dalmatia from early prehistory to the downfall of the national Croatian dynasty.

Novi Sad

Museum of Vojvodina (Vojvodjanski muzej)
The museum was founded in 1947. It is a central museum for all the materials from the region, except sculptures. Thus it is a museum of composite character, and its departments (Archaeological, Ethnographic, Historical) include items of value to any researcher in the cultural history of Vojvodina.

Kragujevac

National Museum (Narodni muzej)
This museum was established in 1950 and is of a composite character. In addition to an important archaeological collection, it possesses collections of coins, art objects, ethnological and historical materials.

Priština

Museum of Kosovo and Metohija (Muzej Kosova i Metohije)
The museum was founded in 1951. It contains systematically arranged collections of Archaeology, Ethnology, History and Natural History. The permanent exhibits represent the culture of Kosovo from early Prehistory to the end of the Middle Ages.

Skopje

Archaeological Museum (Arheološki muzej)
The museum was founded in 1924. It possesses precious archaeological exhibits. The outstanding materials are finds from the great ancient settlements of Macedonia (Skupi, Stobi, Demir Kapija, Čepigovo).

Museum of Contemporary Art (Muzejot no sovremenata umetnost)
The museum was created in 1964 from the numerous contributions sent in by the artists of the entire world to express their solidarity with the city ravaged by earthquake. The permanent exhibition, opened in 1970, contains works of Yugoslav and foreign artists of the 20th century.

SELECTED BIBLIOGRAPHY

BIHALJI-MERIN, OTO. *Art Treasures of Yugoslavia.* (Yugoslavia, Belgrade, 1973).

SREJOVIC, D. Europe's First Monumental Sculpture: New Discoveries at Lepenski Vir. (London, 1972).

MANO-ZISI, DJ. *The Antique in the National Museum in Belgrade.* (Belgrade, 1954).

HOLMQUIST, W. *Germanic Art during the First Millennium, A. D.* (Stockholm, 1955).

KASTELIC, J., MANSUELLI, G., AND KROMER, K. *Situla Art: Ceremonial Bronzes of Ancient Europe.* (London, 1965, 1966).

COROVIC-LJUBINKOVIC, M. *The Icons of Ohrid.* (Belgrade, 1953).

RADOJCIC, S. *Frescoes of Sopocani.* (Belgrade, 1953).

GRABAR, A. *Byzantine Painting.* (Geneva, 1953).

BIHELJI-MERIN, OTO. *Byzantine Frescoes and Icons in Yugoslavia.* (New York, 1960).

WENZEL, M. *Bosnian and Herzegovinian Tombstones: Who Made Them and Why.* ("Südost-Forschungen," XXI, Munich, 1962, pp. 102–43).

BIHELJI-MERIN, OTO, AND BENAC, A. *Bogomil Sculpture.* (New York, 1965).

BIHELJI-MERIN, OTO. *Masters of Naive Art, A History and Worldwide Survey.* (McGraw-Hill, New York, 1979).

TOMASEVIC, NEBOJSA. *The Magic World of Ivan Generalic.* (Rizzoli, New York, 1976).

INDEX OF ILLUSTRATIONS

169

INDEX OF NAMES

GENERAL INDEX